Judy Klipin was born in Johannesburg, South Africa, where she continues to live with her family. Judy specialises in working with people who are experiencing burnout and people who had challenging childhoods (adult children); more often than not these are the same people. She runs an Adult Child Coach Apprenticeship programme for coaches who want to work in this field.

Judy combines her knowledge and skills as a Martha Beck Certified Master Life Coach and a Transactional Analysis practitioner to teach her clients simple, practical and powerful tools that help them to change – not *who* they are, but *how* they are. She coaches, mentors and trains individuals and groups, both in person and through phone and internet coaching.

Judy has a BA and HDipED from the University of the Witwatersrand and a Masters in Social Sciences from Leicester University.

Judy is also the author of *Recover from Burnout: Life Lessons to Regain your Passion and Purpose*.

Find out more at www.judyklipin.com

Recover from your Childhood

Life lessons for the adult child

Judy Klipin

BOOKSTORM

ISBN: 978-1-928257-62-2
e-ISBN: 978-1-928257-63-9

First published by Penguin Books (South Africa) Pty (Ltd) in 2010
This edition published by Bookstorm (Pty) Ltd in 2019

Published by Bookstorm (Pty) Ltd
PO Box 4532
Northcliff 2115
Johannesburg
South Africa
www.bookstorm.co.za

Cover design by mr design
Printed in the USA

In memory of Carl Alberto,
who taught me how to play

Acknowledgements

There are so many people who have helped with the creation of this book. In no particular order of importance, I would like to thank:

My parents. They are no longer present physically but their lessons and legacy will endure endlessly.

Martha Beck – my teacher, mentor and friend – who saw me, and in so doing allowed me to see myself. I am not often at a loss for words, but find it impossible adequately to express my gratitude and delight for her presence in my life.

My family and friends who, individually and collectively, make my world a better place. Thank you for supporting, encouraging, feeding and believing in me.

My clients who are unfeasibly brave and generous in sharing their journeys of transformation and growth with me.

The Bookstorm team, who have generously and thoughtfully helped me to breathe new life into what was originally called

Life Lessons for the Adult Child (published by Penguin in 2010). Reworking the book I wrote 10 years ago has been an interesting and sometimes rather challenging journey for this adult child. I have valued the opportunity to reflect the evolution of my work with adult children through refining and expanding some of my words and ideas. I hope I have managed to retain the simple energy of the book, while enhancing both the content and the manner in which it is delivered.

Author's Note

In the course of writing this book I have presented many of the stories and experiences related to me by my wonderful clients. I have made every effort to respect their privacy and to honour the confidential nature of the coaching relationship through changing their names and other identifying characteristics. I cannot adequately express how grateful I am to them for trusting me with their stories, and for allowing me to witness their regeneration.

The starfish *motif* that you see in some areas of the book is no accident. I chose the starfish as a symbol for the work that I do for two reasons.

The first is that starfish have regenerative qualities – if they lose one of their limbs, they are able to grow another one in its place. The clients that I am honoured to work with share this ability to regenerate and grow new aspects of themselves to replace wounded ones.

The second is in reference to the 'Starfish Story' of the man who was throwing starfish back into the sea early one morning.

When told by a passerby that he would never be able to make a difference because of the sheer number of starfish that were on the beach, the man responded by picking up another starfish, throwing it into the sea, and saying 'I made a difference to that one.'

Foreword

When I met Judy Klipin and began training her in my system of life coaching, she weighed less than my Golden Retriever and was suffering from a high fever that made her flushed and slightly unsteady. Though in her thirties, she looked about twelve. I was slightly shocked when the training began and I realised that inside this apparent 'little girl' was a fiercely intelligent, deeply compassionate, and extremely experienced wise-woman, one of the best coaches I could ever hope to train.

As it turns out, that paradox – the old soul appearing as a small child – was more fitting than either of us knew. After a few years of practicing as a life coach, Judy found herself gravitating towards 'adult children', people whose unpredictable early environments pushed them to precocious maturity, but who sustained a sense of being small and uncertain even as competent adults. If you felt old and tired when you were little and vulnerable, and still feel little and vulnerable as you become more old and tired, you have much to gain from Judy's work. You are the adult child for whom this book was written.

Since she is modest to a fault, Judy is unlikely to tell you how many factors led to her deep understanding of adult children. Her childhood and adolescence spanned the last troubled decades of Apartheid rule in South Africa, a country Judy passionately loves. Before reaching twenty, she'd joined other university students as a determined and courageous anti-Apartheid activist. Like any young scholar, she worried about grades, relationships, and becoming a legal adult, and on top of all that, she was fighting for her country's very uncertain future, in the process deliberately violating the laws of an infamously brutal political system.

During all of this – especially when Judy was detained and questioned for a 'crime' she had actually committed (helping organise a meeting of anti-Apartheid students) – her adult-child ability to stay cool in a crisis served her well. But like all South Africans of her generation, she was left with psychological scars that led her to master or create many of the psychological tools in this book. Intimately familiar with the fear and sorrow that shape the small, powerless members of a system where large, powerful authority figures are unjust, unpredictable, or flawed, Judy (and South Africa as a whole) became models for the way in which adult children are wounded and healed – first by being forced to behave with precocious bravery and intelligence in terrifying circumstances, then by creating safety, relaxing, and compassionately unravelling the knots of anxiety and trauma that formed during a difficult past.

If you are an adult child, for whatever reason, all of this is very good news. Judy's familiarity with your inner condition –

your persistent anxiety, your fear that you're not good enough, your inability to relax, enjoy yourself, trust others, or ask for help – has made her your ideal teacher. In her book you'll find yourself described, explained, and gently introduced to a happier way of being. Judy's psychological logic is unfailingly resonant, her explanations and exercises truly liberating. What feels old and tired in you will grow younger and more carefree. What feels small and broken will become stronger and more confident. I've found comfort and enlightenment in *Recover from your Childhood,* and I know you will too.

Martha Beck

Introduction

I am an adult child.

I was born into a wealthy family. Not owning yachts and islands wealthy, but well-off by anyone's standards. And then, for a whole range of political and economic reasons that were beyond individual control, the wealth wasn't there anymore. My parents and their young family had the Persian carpet ripped out from underneath them. It had a profound impact on them and the family unit.

My parents did the best they could to protect me and my siblings and create a safe environment for us, but what with the financial anxiety and accompanying tensions, and the worry and disappointment with life that lurked constantly on the outskirts of both of their lives, there was unpredictability. This unpredictability was almost perfectly mirrored in my performance at school; sometimes understanding concepts effortlessly and doing well in some tests, and other times not quite getting to grips with what was going on around me in the classroom. I spent a lot of time staring out of the window, lost in a fog of distraction.

What started off as a consequence of a period of upheaval in my home life took on a life of its own and the fear of not doing well enough became a self-fulfilling prophecy for a number of years.

Three times a year for twelve years, I was reminded that my performance was not good enough. It reached a point where it seemed silly to be putting any effort into my school work, because it never seemed to make a difference. With the exception of one or two, none of my teachers was ever satisfied with my effort or with my performance. Obviously, I interpreted this as meaning that it was I who was not good enough.

As a life coach I am lucky enough to work with a wide range of clients. They come to consult me for different reasons and at different stages in their lives. After some time in my practice I began to notice themes and challenges and distinct similarities which were common to many of them, similarities that resonated with me quite strongly.

At first I was slightly taken aback at how many of these people had limiting beliefs that centred on (among other things) their need to be perfect, their inability to trust themselves and others, and their horror of asking for help. Over time I began to realise that these limiting beliefs seemed to stem from childhoods punctuated by inconsistency, unpredictability, and/or varying degrees of physical, emotional and spiritual chaos.

This led me to explore the syndrome of the 'adult child' and to do a lot of reading on the subject. I discovered that, although there have been numerous books written about adult children, none of them were readily available in South Africa, where I live, and that many of them were concerned specifically with 'adult children of alcoholics'.

In my practice I had noticed that not all of my 'adult child' clients came from families with addictions. Many had grown up in families where there were challenges of another kind – depression, chronic illness, living apart from their parents and being raised by more distant family members, being sent to boarding school, etc. Generally, any child who grows up in a family that is unpredictable and/or chaotic in some way and that is unable to provide a consistently nurturing and containing environment, is at risk of growing up to be an adult child. And that accounts for a lot of people! South Africa has a high incidence of adult children because, no matter how 'normal' and predictable the family environment might have been, the macro environment we all grew up in has never been stable or certain. For as far back as anyone can remember, there has been political, social and economic volatility and uncertainty. The vast majority of our population, I believe, has at least some of the characteristics of adult children.

I grew frustrated with the lack of readily available, appropriate and applicable materials that would help my clients make sense of their lives and understand that the sometimes paralysing limiting beliefs that they were victim to were a function of how they grew up, which resulted in this syndrome called 'adult child' rather than as a result of something that they were not doing right, or something that was their fault.

Out of this frustration, my work, my research and, with the help of my clients, this book began to take on its own particular shape and substance. I tried it out in various forms. I built in a number of exercises and included the liberating method of writing things down. I worked through a lot of it with my clients and I shared the experience with people I trust.

The result is a book that has been structured in such a way that it combines information with a range of do-it-yourself coaching tools to help you, the adult child, relate the materials to your own life, and to help you to start identifying how and where to make changes to your thought patterns and your behaviour. While much of the information may not seem new to you, I urge you to read everything carefully and to do the suggested exercises with as much reference to your own life experience as possible. You may find some of the chapters to be easy and liberating, while some sections will be harder and may require some soul searching and honest self-reflection.

Take your time and move at your own pace. I promise you that the journey will be well worth it.

As you work your way through these pages you will be given information that will help you understand what experiences and behaviours make 'adult children' who they are, and the exercises will help you to apply the knowledge and understanding to your own life. The aim of this book is to educate and to empower in order to get you to a point where you can *give yourself permission to make new choices* about how you want to be in the world. A child's choices are limited, but as adults we do have choice in most things that we do, even though it is sometimes hard to remember this. Adult children in particular struggle to feel that they are allowed to make choices for themselves. This book will help you believe that you can.

As you begin to understand more about yourself and why you are the way you are, you will begin to change the way you see yourself and feel about yourself, and ultimately your place in the world. Without changing *who* you are, my hope is that you will be able to change *how* you are.

Getting Started

In reading this book you may experience profound insights and reach a depth of understanding that will help make sense of a less than stellar childhood, but much of the power of *Recover from your Childhood* lies in completing the exercises, and I would encourage you to do them. I have read self-help books too numerous to count, and almost all of them include exercises along the way to help the reader apply what they are reading about and understand the information in relation to their own life and experience. And, I admit, I often skip the exercises or 'do them in my head' rather than actually put pen to paper. I understand that it feels easier to read that way, and if you choose this approach you will certainly still benefit from what you read. If you do complete the exercises, though, I guarantee that it will make the experience richer and more powerful for you.

As Charles L Whitfield says in his book *A Gift to Myself*, 'To get free, we begin to *identify* and *name* a lot of things'. At first this may seem uncomfortable as you have probably spent much of your life ignoring and denying things, so it may take some getting used to. You may also feel that you are revealing your family secret and betraying people you care about (more on that later). Please know that you can 'identify and name' but not necessarily *blame*. Most people, and that includes your parents, do the best they can, no matter how poor that 'best' is. This process is not so much about blaming as it is about understanding. Of course, you may want to apportion some blame for a while and that is also okay, and feelings of anger or resentment may well come up – that is part of the process and you will get past it – but it is not the primary purpose of the exercises.

One of the best and safest ways to 'identify and name' is by writing things down – preferably by hand. I am a big fan of keeping a diary and journaling (Julia Cameron's 'the morning pages' is a favourite tool of mine) because I have seen the healing power of putting pen to paper – both for my clients and in my own experience.

Before you go any further, therefore, I recommend that you find yourself a suitable writing book to use as your journal. I like a hard-covered, ring-bound book that I can write in when I am in bed or in the garden, or anywhere that is peaceful and safe for me and where I can turn inward for a while. Select a pen or pencil that brings you pleasure to write with. You will probably be writing about a lot of emotions and recording information that you may not have told anyone before, not even yourself, so you may want to find a safe and private place to keep your journal between entries.

To start with, I suggest that you write down three goals you would like to achieve through reading this book. Then, when you have finished reading and done all the exercises, come back to the goals and see whether you achieved them. You might, for example, aim to gain better understanding and acceptance of yourself, improve your self-confidence, become more assertive, and improve your relationship.

I also strongly suggest that you set aside some personal time in order to do justice to this process and to fulfil the commitment you have made to yourself. It does not need to be the same time every day or week, but you should make sure you dedicate some uninterrupted hours to go through the materials and do the exercises. You may find that you need to take longer over some of the exercises than others, and that you will want to think about some of the chapters more than others. Listen to your instincts about how and when to do the exercises and the readings. If you feel like you need to slow down or take a break for a few days, then do that.

I'd recommend that you find a safe space to go through these exercises without fear of interruption. You may want to go to a park or into your study or to sit up in your bed to do the work. Anywhere that you feel safe and private will work, somewhere that allows you to forget about the outside world and concentrate on yourself for a while.

Children who grow up in scary or sterile environments learn to numb out the sad and bad feelings, but these feelings do not go away: they just go underground. We process and let go of feelings by *feeling* them and making sense of them. When we numb out the bad we also, unfortunately, numb out the good, so I encourage you to try and become aware of your feelings – both physical and emotional – and make sense of them by *writing* about them in your journal. The exercises are to help you do this. As you complete each exercise, try to identify emotions like happiness, anger, sadness, joy, resentment, guilt, hope, and become more aware of your physical sensations such as cold, heat, pain, pleasure, relaxation, tension, hunger or satisfaction.

Be Present

Write regularly in your journal. If possible, it would be wonderful if you could write what Julia Cameron, author of *The Artist's Way*, refers to as 'the morning pages'. Every morning when you first wake up, pick up your journal and a pen, and write three pages *by hand* of whatever is on your mind. No one will see it and you don't even need to read it to yourself – ever. It is just a way to be still and process what is on your mind. Often it is a load of rubbish and that is okay. In fact, it is great! I find that this is a great exercise for adult children because it shows the benefit of just doing something for the good it does you, without your needing to do it perfectly, make a difference to anyone, or get it right – it is just for YOU. You may feel a little silly at first, but after a couple of days I know you will start to love it and love the clarity it brings to the rest of your day.

After identifying and naming, *sharing* comes next. Sharing with a safe person can be very healing and liberating. Because much of growing up in a family that protects a wounded parent is about keeping the family secret, adult children often find it hard to be honest about their childhoods. The fear of speaking out often relates to feeling as though they are betraying their parents or worrying that they will be horribly rejected if they tell the truth. There is often a childlike fear that telling the truth will result in disaster. I love telling my clients (when it is appropriate of course) that I am adult child. They see that it is okay to own that, and that the consequences will not be dire. Actually, it is more than okay. Every time I say it, I feel a little freer.

You will need to choose someone whom you trust to treat you with care and unconditional love when you tell them your truth. The first time I worked up the courage to tell someone (my first boyfriend) about my less than perfect childhood, he told me that he didn't believe me because my parents were too nice. He was right. My parents were fantastic, amazing people and I loved – and continue to love - them very much. They were clever and quirky and funny and eccentric. They were kind and generous and brave. They were excellent people. But they were wounded, and those wounds made them less than perfect parents. Needless to say, it took another fifteen or so years before I felt ready to try that again!

If you do not feel that you can sufficiently trust anyone whom you already know, it may be a good idea to seek out a therapist or counsellor to speak to.

This may not be an easy journey for you, and what you read here and the exercises you complete will in all likelihood bring up some challenging emotions and memories. I urge you to treat yourself gently and carefully should you find that this is happening to you. If at any point you feel that you are struggling to process these emotions on your own, please do not hesitate to set up an appointment to see a therapist, counsellor or coach who specialises in this area so that they can assist you to feel better and to look after yourself.

You do not have to do this on your own.

1

Adult Children

I suspect that everyone over the age of 18 is, to some extent, an adult child. Adult children are everywhere.

Consider this: if, from a very early age, you felt an unconscious obligation to be a grown up in your family or found yourself, for any of a very large number of reasons, in situations where you didn't feel that you could rely on your parents or primary caregiver consistently and reliably to meet your emotional needs, you are probably an adult child.

To be fair, it is almost impossible for parents to create a perfect childhood for their children, no matter how hard they try. There is a child to adult continuum, and all of us fit somewhere along that line between child and adult, depending on how successfully we have managed to navigate – or had navigated for us – key events in our childhood and adolescence. We also shift along this continuum according to how we feel and how we respond to certain elements in our lives. So, for example, you may be very adult and 'in charge' when you are at your children's parent-teacher meetings, but you may feel very childlike when you walk into a meeting with your boss.

It doesn't really matter what was going on in your family, or why you felt you needed to be the grown up. What matters is that you did.

I work with a wide range of clients in my profession as a life coach, and most of them display, to varying degrees, some or all of the characteristics, limiting beliefs and patterns of behaviour ascribed to the adult child. My clients come from a variety of backgrounds and their childhood dramas and disappointments are of wide-ranging severity; the information I have studied and absorbed on adult children applies differently to each individual client, just as it will to you.

I sometimes use the term 'reluctant hero' in relation to adult children, because they are so brave. As children our choices are limited. We pretty much have to do as we are told and put up with what life gives us. But these children often complete tasks and take emotional responsibility for things that only adults should be expected to do. In my mind they are heroes, although they may not feel like heroes. For them, doing what they need to do may feel like nothing out of the ordinary. They do not ask to be brave but they frequently commit acts of extreme bravery, holding things together for themselves, their siblings, and often for their parents. They do it because they do not have a choice. They are reluctant heroes.

One such reluctant hero is Sam. He is a man in his thirties, soft spoken, and with a slight hesitation in his speech. I like him immediately.

'I must have been about 10 the first time my siblings and I started referring to our parents as "the children",' Sam remembers. 'I was sitting alone at the dining room table trying to make sense of my maths homework, and my older brother walked past and asked, "Where are the children?" We thought it was hilarious and were delighted with how funny we were. But the truth is that we *did* feel like the parents a lot of the time, especially my older brothers, who used to look out for me above and beyond the call of regular brotherly duty.'

Sam has come to consult me because he struggles with feeling competent at work and, although he is very conscientious and does well in his job, he never feels as though he is doing quite well enough. As I get to know him, I discover that he is clever, quick and insightful, but that he never really believes the positive feedback he receives from colleagues and supervisors. His story comes out slowly and across a few sessions.

Sam and his brothers grew up in a family that had some challenges. Despite their best efforts, his parents were unable to provide the kind of safe, loving, consistent and predictable home environment that children require to thrive and grow up to be healthy and robust adults. Although they loved their children, they were not always able to notice and appreciate them through their own pain and anxiety. Sam and his brothers were often left to look after their own and each others' needs. In many respects, Sam did not have a happy and carefree childhood; from an early age he learned to be serious, to be responsible and reliable, and to be self-sufficient.

I learn to know a man who is understated, anxious (but tries hard to hide it), sensitive, intuitive, still reliable, more responsible and fiercely independent. As we work carefully together I also learn that his intimate relationships have always been a source of discomfort for him; he always seems to choose the wrong partner and stays in unhealthy relationships far longer than many others would. He is a living embodiment of the limiting belief I call 'If I were better, it would be better.'

Sam is a fairly typical example of the many adult child clients I work with, so much so that he is among many who refer to their parents as their 'children'.

There are many, many children who grow up in an environment that is unstable and feels unsafe and unpredictable. As adults these people generally share a range of behaviours, beliefs and concerns that characterise reluctant heroes, and that make their journey through life less than carefree at best, a downright struggle at worst.

Mark is another example, another reluctant hero. He is a large man and has a commanding presence. At first meeting he can be a little intimidating, but when you get to know him better, he reveals himself as a gentle giant.

Mark had what looked to the outside world to be a perfect childhood. But inside the home his father gave vent to his anger and frustrations in temper tantrums that used to leave the windows rattling in their frames, and the family in tatters of fear and distress. A very well respected doctor, Mark's dad used to take advantage of his medical knowledge and easy access to medicines, and abuse prescription medication. The strong painkillers he took every day fuelled his rages, and he would threaten violence frequently.

Although he very seldom actually became violent, the danger was always there and Mark became adept at reading the signs and intervening to take his father's attention away from his mother or younger sister. Mark would always be alert to opportunities to distract his father from his rage, while his younger sister would stay out of the way as much as possible – and try to disappear so that she would not be on the receiving end of her father's rage and violence.

Now an adult, Mark is a very responsible, caring and considerate man, always trying to avoid conflict and to make peace where there might be anger. At work he is the person who is sent into the meetings that could turn nasty. His sister is a shy woman, never drawing attention to herself, always doing her best to stay out of the limelight. She has not had a promotion at work for ten years but, as she hasn't got into any trouble either, she is happy with that. Neither of these two people is reaching his and her full potential, because they are limited by the numerous unconscious fears and beliefs that hold them back and restrict them from leading the lives they should be leading.

In my coaching practice I regularly work with clients who are adult children, and I have found that there are almost as many different contexts for the adult child as there are adult children. Some of the conditions or circumstances that give rise to this syndrome include:

* addiction or substance abuse by a parent or sibling
* financial worries
* a special needs child in the family
* chronic physical or mental illness or depression of any family member, but particularly a parent
* being sent to boarding school
* the early death of a parent or parents
* absence of one or both parents for any considerable length of time or periods of time

Any or all of these conditions may – and very often do – result in children who were very responsible and reliable, who were little grown-ups in a family that did not have adequate, reliable or consistent adult role models.

As adults, these adult children tend to carry with them the fears and insecurities they experienced as children and, when feeling vulnerable or insecure, they will often, despite being grown up and mature, 'regress' to behaviours and beliefs that were developed when they were growing up in an unreliable environment.

Often, too, it seems that the syndrome gets passed down through the generations. Some of my clients can't quite put their finger on what the unhappiness in their family might have been that has resulted in their adult child tendencies. This is confusing to them because they remember their parents as happy, consistent and functional. After some time, though, they may realise that their grandparents – the parents of a parent or even both parents – had some habit or behaviour that created unpredictability or fear in the home (substance abuse, a vicious temper, depression, even post traumatic stress from being involved in a war). And so, even though my clients' childhoods seem to have been healthy and happy, they begin to realise that their parent/s were themselves adult children.

Understanding that the experience of having been very responsible and reliable in childhood, coupled with the inclination to revert to often fear-based childlike responses in adulthood, is important for grown-up men and women to make sense of how and why they relate to the world, themselves and others the way they do. Children who take on adult responsibilities usually take life very seriously and often struggle to have fun and enjoy themselves. And adults who revert to childlike behaviours find it hard to navigate conflicts, work, romantic relationships, authority and many other aspects of adulthood. So, being an adult child is often a double whammy that affects those of us who grew up in less than perfect circumstances.

Neither childhood nor adulthood were or are comfortable places to be.

It is far from all bad, however. There are many gifts and advantages that come with being an adult child. Adult children are often very insightful, very dependable, intuitive, empathic, sensitive, kind, generous and creative. Many of the characteristics that drive adult children to be the best they can be result in incredible talents and abilities.

Through deepening the understanding of what makes an adult child and how they operate in the world, and identifying areas for changing behaviours and attitudes, it is possible to harness the strengths and ameliorate the weaknesses of adult children and set them free to fulfil their enormous potential. I know, because I see it happening every day in my coaching practice.

Try this exercise and you will see what I mean.

Describe Yourself

Turn to a clean page in your journal and draw a line down the middle of it. In the left-hand column, write a list of all the 'weaknesses' or challenges you see in yourself. It may look something like this:

My weaknesses	
I leave everything to the last minute I get tired very easily I get sick often	

Once you have filled that side of the page with as many insights about yourself that you regard as negative, write down all the positive aspects of yourself in the right-hand column.

My weaknesses	My Strengths
I leave everything to the last minute I get tired very easily I get sick often	I get a lot done quickly I work well under pressure I am reliable I am empathetic I have a strong intuition I care about people

After you have captured all the strengths that you can think of – you can add more to both columns as you think of new points to put down – see if there are any links. Do any of your strengths relate to your weaknesses? For instance, I get a lot done quickly and work well under pressure precisely because I procrastinate and leave everything to the last minute. Similarly, my sensitivity which makes me tire easily and get run down if I am not careful, is also the reason I am so good at my job. My empathy and ability to 'hear' the unspoken things that my clients are telling me is what makes me a good coach.

Our weaknesses and strengths are often different sides of the same coin. Choosing which side of the coin to embrace and expose can radically transform how we see ourselves.

What Makes an Adult Child?

Anyone who grew up in a family that was not always and consistently 'happy and healthy', or was raised by parents who grew up in families that were not 'happy and healthy', may show a predisposition to adult child thoughts and behaviours to varying degrees. As I have said before, the idea of a 'healthy' family is pretty flawed in and of itself, but it is helpful to have an understanding of the differences between families that produce adults and those that produce adult children.

'Healthy' families help and support children and family members in their development by providing a safe space to grow and experiment with boundaries, and by providing positive role models for relationships.

Children learn how to be in the world by watching the grown-ups; observing how they relate to each other in their intimate relationships, and to other adults in their lives. They also experience how adults relate to their own children. If a child's parents have difficult relationships with each other as well as with their children, those children will grow up not knowing how to be in an easy relationship.

'Healthy' families do experience times of chaos and crisis, but

they generally stay in these for a relatively short time before returning to the normal containing environment.

'Unhealthy' families tend to either remain in a constant state of crisis, or lurch from one crisis to the next, with brief and uncertain periods of 'normality' in between. It is this lack of predictability, the chaos and the sometimes frightening situations which give rise to many of the limiting beliefs and behaviours exhibited by adult children.

Shame and secrecy, which often accompany parental dysfunction such as addiction or anti-social behaviour, may result in feelings of self-blame and guilt in the child, as well as fears around not being 'good enough'. *Denial or protection of the family secret(s) often results in the adult child denying or neglecting his or her own emotions, feelings and needs.* All the emotional energy goes into trying to hold things together and keeping up appearances. Often this is achieved by stifling the natural emotions, fears and desires experienced by the child.

The reality is that if the children in an unhappy home had allowed themselves to see and feel the truth of how bad it really felt, the situation may have been intolerable for them. As adults, we can leave a situation that we are not enjoying (although doing this is often hard for adult children for reasons we will get to in a little while) but it is not possible for children to physically remove themselves from negative situations. They can remove themselves emotionally, though, and this often results in the development of a coping mechanism of mental and emotional numbing to keep out negative feelings.

Sadly, this coping mechanism tends to keep the good feelings out too.

The feelings are still there, though, even if they are being ignored. If adult children do not allow themselves to acknowledge their emotional discomfort, sadness or anger can often be somatised into physical symptoms. This frequently results in stress-related illnesses. Wayne Kritsberg, writing in *The Adult Children of Alcoholics Syndrome,* identifies a wide range of physical disorders resulting from growing up in a high-stress environment.

The following ailments cited by Kritsberg and slightly adapted here by me, are common to adult children and range in intensity from mild discomfort to severely disabling. See if any of them sound familiar to you:

* tense shoulders (from feelings of carrying a huge burden) and headaches
* lower back pain (a feeling of being unsupported in life)
* gastro-intestinal disorders such as ulcers, heartburn, IBS etc (ignoring your 'gut feelings')
* colds and flu
* difficulty sleeping
* low energy and fatigue
* allergies and sinusitis
* sexual dysfunction

My adult child clients sometimes think that I am psychic when I suggest that they may benefit from going to have back and shoulder massages, but I know that most adult children have sore necks and shoulders for much of their lives, so much so that they sometimes aren't even aware of the discomfort because it has just become a part of them. Releasing the physical tension and trauma held in the muscles is a useful and often comforting way to start releasing emotional pain and trauma.

Go for a massage

If you are an adult child, chances are you experience physical tension and/or some degree of chronic ailment such as allergies, sinusitis, headaches or digestive problems. Having some sort of body work done, be it a massage, reflexology or physiotherapy, will help to release the emotional discomfort and lessen the physical discomfort, too.

Children in unpredictable home situations frequently feel invisible and fear being forgotten. There may be a tendency to get sick, often in an (unconscious) attempt to have some attention paid to them. Perhaps the only time they really feel noticed and thought about is when they are ill. It is extremely frightening for children to feel a sense of invisibility. Small children in particular believe that they are the centre of the world and that everything happens in relation to them: bad things happen because they are not good enough and good things happen because they are. If they are not being thought about, the childish fear is that their world – and therefore *the* world – may fall apart.

In an unpredictable family, bad things *do* often happen, resulting in lots of feelings of badness on the part of the child.

13

This can result in what I call the 'if I were better, it would be better' syndrome. Children in these families unconsciously (or even consciously) believe that if they were just a good child, did everything right, didn't cause trouble, were clever and perfect, then things would be okay. This belief spills over into adulthood, resulting in super-responsible, super-reliable grown-ups who develop unconscious limiting beliefs that if they don't do everything perfectly then something bad and potentially catastrophic might happen.

Adult children often have a need to be needed in order to ensure that they will not be forgotten about. So they will find themselves at the centre of a crisis, indispensable at work, and/or at the beck and call of friends and family, sometimes even acquaintances, around the clock. Strangely, they can also vacillate between being needy and clingy, and being very self-sufficient and not asking for help or relying on anyone to look after them, while going out of their way to look after others.

The compulsion to make things better by being better, coupled with the need to be needed, contribute enormously to adult children pushing themselves into exhaustion and overwhelm. In combination with a real struggle to say no or ask for help, it is easy to see why so many adult children experience burnout.

The denial, shame and secrecy that so many children who grew up in chaotic families internalise from an early age often manifests later as an inability to listen to, and to honour, their own need and wants. The lack of acknowledgement of their own observations, feeling and reactions results in many adult children taking on codependent behaviours.

In her book, *Codependent No More*, Melody Beatty describes codependence:

'A codependent person is one who has let another person's behaviour affect him or her, and who is obsessed with controlling that person's behaviour.'

Originally the term 'codependence' referred to spouses or partners of people with chemical dependency issues (they were the codependent partner) but further studies have shown that it is much broader than that. Charles Whitfield refers to codependence as 'a disease of lost selfhood' – it results from concentrating on the needs of others at our own expense.

Although the concept is very useful in helping to understand why so many people get into and stay in relationships that are fraught with disappointment, drama and sometimes even danger, because of its association with addiction recovery I prefer to refer to codependency as 'others-centredness.'

Others-centredness is exactly what it sounds like; the propensity to put others at the centre of our focus and attention, and ourselves on the periphery of our own lives. We learn how to be by watching the grown-ups and if we see others-centredness around us when we are children, that is how we start to be in our own lives and relationships.

People who are otherscentred often become so focused on the needs of the important people in their life that they forget about their own needs. 'If I were better, it would be better' is bizarrely true when it comes to others-centredness. If adult children who are otherscentred are able to put themselves at the centre of their own lives and start paying more attention to their own needs and wants, things really will get better.

While my coaching of adult children is not meant as a substitute for psychotherapy, and I do not spend too much time understanding childhood behaviours and patterns, it is important to acknowledge the past and the impact it has had on the present in order to change the future. Understanding the impact of various childhood events is a way to make it easier for clients to identify and understand some of the limiting beliefs that are affecting their lives every day.

None of us has reached where we are in our lives today through following a linear path. Instead our journey is likely to have had many twists along the way, all adding to the richness and complexity that make us the multi-faceted people that we are.

Here is another useful exercise.

The Tree of Life

Take a few minutes to think of some of the key events in your life so far. Starting as far back as you can remember, make some brief notes of all the good and the bad things that have happened to you. For some people very profound events which would influence their lives might have taken place while they were in the womb. If you are one of those people, write that down too. Now take a new sheet of paper and draw these events as circles spreading out from the first core event that you identified. Draw the good events in one colour, and the hard events in another colour. Just like the rings of a tree illustrate the good years and the harder years that the tree has lived through, this exercise will show you how the good and bad times have led you, in ever increasing circles, to where you are now (and beyond). Can you see how not all the events were bad? And that those that were bad, usually precede good ones?

For example: dark ring: had to move house when I was 7. Light ring: met a gang of wonderful friends who lived in the new neighbourhood. Dark ring: scary times at university due to anti-apartheid activities. Light ring: met Nelson Mandela two days after he was released from jail while a student involved with anti-apartheid activities.

As you work through this book, you may want to add things to this picture, events that you remember or that come to mind while you are completing some of the exercises. Perhaps you would like to illustrate the importance of a particular event by marking it in some way. I use this exercise to help people make sense of all the important events, both good and bad, that have happened in their lives, and how they have helped to shape them into the person they are today. Remember the time you were given a doll instead of the promised bicycle for your birthday? This may be why you are so good at keeping promises and honouring commitments today. Ever thought about that?

Are you an Adult Child?

When someone does something to disappoint you, do you feel responsible?

Do you struggle to ask for help?

Whenever I meet a new client and I suspect they may be an adult child, I ask these two questions, both of which point to behaviours that are very common to adult children.

Do you find that you take responsibility for everything – every thought, every action, every emotion, every mood – in yourself and in the people around you?

And when you are let down by someone, rather than feeling disappointed in the person who has let you down, do you feel disappointed in yourself and feel that you should have done something differently to avoid the distress? As part of the 'if I were better, it would be better' phenomenon, adult children tend to take responsibility for all the bad things that happen to them and around them.

There are many reasons adult children hate asking for help. They do not want to be a burden, or they worry they may be rejected. Often, also, they don't trust that anyone else can do as good a job as they can. More often than not, though, it just does not occur to them to ask for help.

Sheila is a sprightly 63-year-old, grey haired, smallish and very unassuming. She has been a single parent to her two children since her alcoholic husband left them 20 years ago when the children were both under ten years old. In all this time, she has been a full-time mother, held down a high pressure job and been active in her community. Whenever she comes into my coaching room, the relief at not having to hold everything together for the hour that she is there is evident in the way she snuggles into the couch and wraps her hands around her cup of mint tea. I am fairly sure that these are the only cups of tea that she has not had to make for herself in a very long time.

She has come to me for some coaching because her youngest child has just left home and she is feeling lonely and worried about how she is going to adjust to an empty house. She is thinking about retiring from the job she has had for almost three decades. She tells me she is tired and could do with the change of pace, but she is also scared of the impact that not having somewhere to go every day will have on her. She is, I think, scared that she may disappear. Like so many adult children she has an unconscious need to be needed and noticed, and she is afraid of being forgotten about if she is not playing a specific role. Now that she does not have to be a mother to her children in the same way that she used to, the thought of leaving her job and not being relied upon there either is terrifying. What makes it even harder is that she isn't conscious of these fears.

As she talks about herself she berates herself repeatedly: 'I could have been a better mother, but I really think I did the best I could,' she says over and over again. 'I wish I had had more time for my children, I made sure I went to all their school plays and sports matches, but I couldn't provide them with a father's influence. I should have given them more robust attention, taken them on hikes and adventure holidays maybe. But that is just not me, and I really did do the best I could.' Sheila is clearly very emotional and I can see the tears welling up when she says: 'My relationship with my oldest child is very strained. If I had the chance again I might do some things differently. But I really did the best I could ...'

Perhaps I am just very sensitised to adult children, but it seems to me that Sheila is a prime example of one. As she is from a generation that doesn't talk about themselves and their families as easily as those of us born after 1960 do, I know I need to proceed quite gently and cautiously.

'Tell me, Sheila,' I say, 'you strike me as being a very self-sufficient woman. Do you sometimes struggle to ask for help?' I can see an internal debate going on as Sheila tries to work out what I want the answer to be. Eventually she opts for honesty and nods.

'Yes. I don't even think about asking for help most of the time. I just get on with things. I learned long ago that I needed to do things myself.'

'Okay' I say. 'And when someone disappoints you, do you tend to feel responsible?'

I love this question – for some reason it is a real opening of the Pandora's box that is the adult child. 'Yes!' says Sheila. 'I always think that *I* should have done something differently. I always feel guilty when I am let down.'

With further discussion Sheila reveals a childhood that was indeed unpredictable and chaotic, and she was relieved to hear that her anxieties and feelings of not being good enough were not peculiar to her. She came to realise that rather than it being she who was not good enough, it was the context within which she had been a child that had shaped the way she saw and felt about herself. And that this had made her an adult child.

As soon as Sheila learned to separate herself from her past, she recognised that many of her fears and insecurities had developed in response to what was going on around her in her childhood. She was quickly able to start seeing herself honestly and to recognise that, although she may not have always been perfect, she had certainly managed to be more than good enough most of the time.

Once people have a name for *who* or *what* they are, it makes it relatively easy to help them understand *how* and *why* they are the way they are, and to give them tools and skills to change those thoughts and actions that are not serving them anymore. Knowledge and insight help adult children to change, not *who* they are, but *how* they are.

Are You an Adult Child?

- ★ Do you feel responsible when someone disappoints you?
- ★ Do you struggle to ask for help?

Think of some ways where you may think you have behaved like

- ★ an adult when you were a child, and
- ★ a child since you have been an adult

Can you think of lost opportunities from when you were a child? Can you identify situations that now, as an adult, bring out the child in you? I will always remember the response of one my clients, a wonderful, bubbly and energetic mother of three who, when asked if she ever felt like a child as an adult responded, 'I still can't believe they let me drive a car!'

Write down your examples on a page in your journal, and keep space for other situations that may occur to you as you go along.

As Martha Beck explains in her book *Finding Your Own North Star,* our living space is a pretty accurate reflection of how we feel about our lives. Asking clients to describe their homes is a useful tool for coaches to get a sense of how their clients are feeling about their lives. I use the tool in a different way: by asking my clients to describe the home they grew up in.

When we are children we live in the space created by our parents, or the adults who are looking after us, a space that is reflective of how well they are managing in the world. When I ask clients to describe their childhood homes to me, we get a sense of what growing up must have been like for them. It is very illuminating.

Describe your childhood home

Before reading any further (you will spoil it for yourself if you do) take a few minutes – three or four should be enough – and write down a description in your journal of the home or homes you lived in when you were growing up. Don't think too deeply. Just write what comes to mind, using adjectives in your descriptions. Here is part of the description one of my clients gave me of her childhood home:

'My first home was big and spacious and light. It had a huge garden and I was always playing outside with the neighbourhood children. The bedrooms were all close together and the house was very sunny and warm. Then we moved into a house that was the same size but much more spread out. My parents' bedroom was very far away from our rooms. The garden was much smaller and was very overgrown. There were big trees outside the windows which made the rooms very dark. It was very cold in winter and the floors were uncarpeted and freezing.'

Now read over the description and see what the dominant emotions were that accompanied your description. What were your adjectives? Did you find yourself using words like dark, damp, dreary, cramped? The way you experienced your childhood home or homes is probably the way you experienced your childhood. If you grew up in a house that you remember as warm and sunny in summer but freezing and dark in winter, maybe you had a childhood that had periods of comfort and relaxation and happiness, interspersed with times of sadness and emotional coldness?

What I interpreted from my client's description of her home confirmed what I knew about that client from working with her for some weeks. She had a relatively happy early childhood. There had been a great sense of emotional freedom and she felt very contained by her family and her parents. Her early childhood felt warm and bright. But then something happened to the family and her parents became more distant from their children. There was less emotional freedom and less sense of play and childhood. The client's life began to feel darker and there were periods of emotional coldness and discomfort. Something was happening in the family to block out the happiness and light.

What Does it Mean if You are an Adult Child?

Being an adult child has an impact on both the childhood and the adulthood of the person concerned. Behaving in a very responsible and reliable way from early on in life robs the adult child of a childhood, but the behaviours adopted in an unhappy childhood may also prevent the grown up from feeling mature and able in an adult world.

'I know you are going to find this hard to believe,' says Grant, outwardly a very composed man who holds a senior management position in his company, 'but I am really anxious a lot of the time.'

I am sure that many of his colleagues would be amazed to know that this person who seems so calm and in command actually feels scared and out of his depth much of the time, but I don't find it hard to believe at all. I hear this statement, or something along these lines, frequently from my clients. I relate to it personally, too. Every so often I run into someone I went to university with and when we talk about our student days I frequently hear that I always seemed to be so calm and peaceful to them. If only they knew the constant anxiety I suffered from, the fear of not being good enough, the ever present worry that I was going to fail all my courses (not helped by my willingness to procrastinate and skip lectures in favour of political meetings), or the fact that I was plagued by constant headaches and stomach-aches. And worst of all, the belief that I was the only one who felt like that.

Many adult children feel they are unique in the concerns and anxieties they're burdened with, and believe that they are the only ones who think and feel the way they do. But there are many, many traits, behaviours and limiting beliefs that are common to most adult children.

Janet Geringer Woititz did pioneering work with adult children of alcoholics (ACoA). Although not all (in fact it is only the tip of a very large iceberg) adult children had an alcoholic parent or parents, the defining characteristics that she identified in her research as being common to many adult children of alcoholics, also apply to many adult children. Please bear in mind that the list I'm about to share with you is not an exhaustive nor scientifically developed one, but rather one that Woititz arrived at through years of work with many adult children. Not all of these statements or descriptions will apply fully to each person. Some of them may be only somewhat applicable to you and many will seem interrelated.

One of the defining features of being an 'ACoA', and by extension an adult child, is feeling different and, as Woititz described it, **'guessing what normal is'**, because they do not have an experience of 'normal' – whatever that is. They grew up in an environment that was 'abnormal' and their role models were often not positive. Most adult children think that 'everyone else' is normal and has a perfect family. As most families are on their best behaviour when they have guests, any visits to friends' homes probably reinforced this belief.

In addition to not having a 'normal' family experience, adult children also struggle to know what 'normal' behaviour is and 'normal' emotions are. Adult children like Grant, for instance, often think that they are the only person who is anxious and confused; that everyone else somehow has the answer, when they don't even know what the question is. If they grew up in a family that encouraged secrecy to hide a problem such as a parent's drinking, or depression, or anger or maybe even a scandal of some kind, the adult child often struggles with honesty, open communication and trust in both people and processes.

Adult children have difficulty following projects through from beginning to end

According to Woititz, this is because of the unfulfilled promises that are common in a typical dysfunctional home. Promises and commitments were often not met, and projects were started but not completed, either left by the wayside in favour of another idea or forgotten about completely. So there was no effective modelling of identifying, planning, and executing a project. As a result, in adulthood, problem solving and planning skills are often lacking in the adult child. 'Adult children judge themselves without mercy,' is another characteristic that combines with this one to sometimes make it hard for adult children to finish what they start. Expecting too much of themselves means that many adult children give up on projects before they have given themselves a chance to learn how to do them well. There may also be a tendency to procrastinate, usually because of a need to do everything perfectly. The unnecessary and relentless pressure that many adult children place themselves under to be 'the best' can be immobilising, resulting in leaving a task to the last minute when there is no other alternative but to complete it as well as possible in the short time available. This also provides a handy 'out' in case the end result is not perfect. This way they can say, 'Well, what did you expect? I only had three hours to write that 15-page report.'

Adult children often lie, when it would be just as easy to tell the truth

This does not necessarily mean only big, important lies, but includes 'white' lies – seemingly unimportant untruths aimed at either presenting the adult child in a better light, or promising to make life smoother.

In the early days of the coaching relationship when a client is a few minutes late for their session, they often tell me they are late because of the traffic, or because their boss made them do something before they could leave the office. In time, and with growing self-awareness and trust in themselves and me, they start to say things like 'I lost track of time' or 'I wanted to finish off a task I was busy with.' This subtle shift towards taking responsibility and feeling secure enough to show me that they are not perfect is an important turning point, and when this happens I know that I will soon have a coaching slot opening up for a new client.

Not telling the truth is central to many dysfunctional families where there is often an unspoken rule that the family secret is not to be acknowledged within the family, let alone spoken about outside of the family. That lying is acceptable is demonstrated to children through covering-up, denial, inconsistencies and unreliable behaviour.

Children raised in unhappy families learn not to trust as well as not to tell the truth. The prospect of telling their truth can be terrifying. What if they get punished or get hurt for telling the truth? And so they minimise the truth: 'It wasn't that bad' or 'Plenty of people had a much worse time than I did, I was actually quite lucky.' Sound familiar?

Not only do they learn to keep the truth from others, but they learn to lie to themselves as well.

Adult children also lie to themselves in more practical ways. They tell themselves they don't need help, when they do. They allow themselves to believe that they are not tired, or sick, or hungry or angry or resentful, when they are. They convince themselves that they are responsible for everyone and everything around them.

Adult children judge themselves without mercy

In some families the children may be overtly made to feel not good enough and to be the cause of their parent's unhappiness, while in other families it may be a responsibility that they assume for themselves ('If I were better, it would be better'). Either way, those feelings get internalised and result in adult children being extremely harsh on themselves, and always carrying with them a sense of not being good enough.

'I remember my mother lying on her bed,' Helen tells me, 'kicking her legs in a tantrum and saying, "It's because of you children that I am so unhappy." I was seven.'

Helen is just one of the many adult child clients I have had who have shared similar experiences such as this one with me.

As it is not possible to meet the very high expectations they place on themselves, adult children are constantly disappointed in their own performance. Whatever they do and achieve is never quite enough. They also tend to hang onto a very negative self-image, even in the face of contradictory evidence. (If an adult child were to win the Nobel Prize, he or she would probably say, 'It was nothing; anyone could have done it.')

Another manifestation of this characteristic is feeling responsible if anything goes wrong or if they are disappointed or let down by something or someone. Again, it is a case of 'If I were better, it would be better'. And if things do go right, it is because of someone else or just plain luck.

Adult children often find it hard to trust when good things happen to them; when they land a good job or find a nice partner, for example. They are so used to being disappointed and to feeling not good enough that they can spoil these opportunities by being distrustful and self-sabotaging.

Adult children have a hard time having fun, and they take themselves very seriously

Children of unhappy families do not have a lot of fun. They are constantly walking on eggshells, trying to prevent bad things from happening and anticipating and averting danger. They also don't often witness their parents having fun, so they don't learn about being silly and carefree by watching others.

Children in unhappy families often take on an adult role and feel as though they are the grown-ups and need to feel and to act responsibly. Letting their guard down is scary and may feel uncontaining. Children of these families have a great sense of dignity and pride, and appearing silly, stupid or irresponsible can be unthinkable for them. As Janet Woititz observes, the pressure to be an adult prevents the child from being recognised and acknowledged.

Because they are so responsible and are very seldom silly and playful, adult children are often dream employees because they take themselves and their jobs very seriously. Taking themselves and their jobs seriously is brilliant for bosses and career progression, but it is not great for work–life balance or rest and recreation. This is another reason so many adult children fall prey to exhaustion and burnout.

Adult children have trouble with intimate relationships

Adult children crave normal, healthy relationships and, paradoxically, often struggle with them immensely. We learn how to be in the world by watching our parents and our families. We see how our parents behave with each other, and we experience how they behave with us. Children in unhappy families may have no frame of reference for what a healthy relationship looks like, and their own experience of relating to their parents can be confusing and unpredictable. Rather than demonstrating what a positive relationship looks and feels like, wounded parents often model frightening, disappointing, hurtful, unfulfilling and/or dishonest relationships, with each other and with their children. Many adult children are terrified of conflict, which is a normal part of any relationship. They feel so underequipped to deal with conflict, they often avoid it or overreact to it.

As a result many adult children vacillate between being needy and pushing their partners away – what Woititz describes as 'I want you – go away'. The fear of abandonment or disappointment is so great that adult children find it hard to trust, and they may overreact to the minor disagreements or disappointments which are part and parcel of all relationships.

This fear of abandonment, coupled with a negative self-image, can make it hard for the adult child to believe that anyone would actually want to be with them. Consequently, they can feel that being left is inevitable and so may accelerate the process by pushing their partner away so as to get the abandonment over and done with. Alternatively, adult children may put pressure on the relationship to progress very quickly, in order to reassure themselves that they are wanted and needed. Adult children may also find themselves in unsuitable relationships.

Adult children overreact to situations over which they have no real control

Children raised in unhappy environments live in a state of dread and anticipation of bad things happening. Because their parents are not in control, the children do not experience a controlled environment. To survive the chaos and unpredictability, children in these settings develop a need to take charge and to know what to expect. Something as simple as a minor change to a social arrangement, being kept waiting in the doctor's rooms, or even the supermarket running out of a favourite comfort food, can ruin an adult child's day.

Adult children have learned to trust themselves rather than others, and to rely on no one else. This can come across as being controlling and rigid. They are like this not because they don't want to hear other people's input, but because the fear of sudden and uncertain change that is not controlled by them, is so frightening.

Adult children constantly seek approval and affirmation from others

Children see themselves through the eyes of their primary caregivers (or, rather, the way they perceive their primary caregivers see them). If they do not receive the unconditional love, encouragement and positive reinforcement that is so critical to the development of healthy self-esteem, they may become confused about how important and valuable they are. Adult children, so often not adequately 'seen' in childhood, often become approval junkies, constantly needing to be noticed and appreciated by others. A way that adult children get affirmation is by making themselves indispensable – if they are needed then their value will be proven.

It seems to be contradictory, yet when affirmation is given, it is often hard for adult children to believe and accept this affirmation. I use an appreciation exercise in group work where I ask clients what they appreciate in themselves. It is usually a struggle for them to identify more than three or four things they appreciate about themselves, but when I ask them what they appreciate in their fellow participants, well then the comments come rolling off their tongues. And get deflected.

'Jane, I really appreciate your bravery,' says John.

'No, John, I am not brave at all. YOU are the brave one', is how the conversation often goes.

It can be so much easier to see in others what we struggle to see in ourselves.

Adult children have a hard time feeling comfortable and feel they are different from other people

Adult children tend to think that everyone else knows how to behave or how to feel and that they are the only ones who feel out of their depth or uncomfortable in an unfamiliar setting.

What they don't realise is that there are many, many other adult children who are also feeling uncomfortable and out of their depth.

Keeping secrets makes children careful about what they talk about, and having an uncomfortable home life can discourage children from inviting friends over, often resulting in uneasy social relationships, or isolation and loneliness.

Adult children often feel different from other people and, in reality, many adult children *are* different from other people. They have felt different since their childhood. Their life experience has resulted in them developing a whole set of characteristics, behaviours and beliefs that are quite particular.

Adult children are often very sensitive, very intuitive and have a great deal of empathy. Their sensitivity and thin-skinnedness can make them feel very uncomfortable, particularly when they are around people who are not comfortable themselves. Many of my clients are what Dr Judith Orloff, a psychiatrist and author of the book *Positive Energy*, calls 'intuitive empaths' – they can literally *feel* the emotions that people they are close to are experiencing. They may resist going to visit an old friend because they always leave feeling depressed and disappointed with the world, not realising that they are carrying their friend's feeling of depression and disappointment away with them. Because they are mostly unaware of what is happening to them, they feel like there is something wrong with them.

Adult children are either irresponsible, or incredibly responsible

Adult children often grew up in families that did not model sharing responsibility and working together as a team. In addition, the child often takes responsibility for the family and assumes the role of an adult. So the inclination of adult children is either to do it all (super-responsible) because it is what they are used to doing, or to do nothing (super-irresponsible) because they had enough of being responsible in their childhoods.

I used to think, in my adult-child, black-or-white, all-or-nothing way, that this characteristic meant that adult children were either completely irresponsible, or completely responsible. All or nothing, one or the other. But I have come to realise that adult children can be both irresponsible and responsible at the same time. Often, they are super responsible in relation to everyone and everything around them, while being super irresponsible towards themselves. They will make sure that everyone else's needs are met, while failing to meet their own. Their 'others-centredness' ensures that they put everyone else at the centre of their focus and attention, and their own needs become peripheral to them.

Adult children also find it hard to set boundaries and to say No. They don't have a good sense of their own limitations. Often this manifests in adult children taking on too many projects or accepting too many commitments, and feeling that they have to do everything perfectly. They pressure themselves to hold down high-powered jobs, be active members of their community, go to all their children's school functions, take care of their ageing parents, be the perfect supportive spouse and friend, and look after their health.

Even if they resent some or all of these responsibilities, they keep on with them. My adult child clients often arrive in my room on the brink of or in full-blown burnout, exhausted by forcing themselves to do perfectly even the things they hate.

Zanele was a good example. One glance at her and I knew that this was a perfectionist extraordinaire. From the top of her beautifully braided head to the tips of her designer stilettos, this woman was very carefully put together and very carefully held together. She was like a jack-in-the-box, waiting for the lid to be lifted. During her first session she admitted she hated her job so much she would take off all her work clothes on the front step when she got home and walk through the door naked because she didn't want to contaminate her home with work (a clue that she had been ignoring for years).

She wept bitter tears of sadness and regret when she thought about how she had gone into work that she hated rather than what she really wanted to do, which was to be a teacher. But teachers don't earn as much money as bankers, and she had always felt the need to be the breadwinner for her extended family. The realisation of how she had sold herself short, and the fear of what might happen to her if she allowed herself to not be super-responsible was so overwhelming that she scuttled out the door at the end of the session, never to return.

Adult children are intensely loyal even when it is obvious that their loyalty may be misplaced

Unhappy families seem to result in great loyalty. Members of the family stay put long after they could objectively and understandably leave. The inability to leave may be due to fear and insecurity, or even fear of failure, rather than strength and devotion. Even when the going gets tough, there is nowhere else to be.

Children raised in these families do not have the wherewithal, emotional or material, to leave a situation that is not working for them. Instead, they feel compelled to make excuses for the dysfunction and disappointment, and they live in the hope that things will get better if they can just be good, do the right things, look after everybody and make things better.

Adult children will act this out in their personal and professional lives, and make excuses for bad or disappointing behaviour in others over and over again. This explains why adult children stay so long in situations – jobs, relationships, friendships, gym contracts – that are no longer serving them.

Adult children are impulsive and often lock themselves into a course of action without giving serious consideration to alternative behaviours or possible consequences.

They may, for example, accept extra responsibility at work, agree to do something on a whim, or even impulsively suggest an outlandish idea like climbing Mount Everest with friends. Even when it becomes clear that it is not such a great idea (maybe there just isn't enough time, they realise they are terrified of heights, or that they hate their job), adult children will find it extremely difficult to allow themselves to change their minds and to make new choices.

These characteristics and descriptions are by no means exhaustive, and not all of them apply to every adult child. Each individual has their own set of characteristics and behaviours that manifest in their own individual way. But I have yet to meet anyone for whom not one of these characteristics is recognisable or applicable.

Having read these eleven characteristics (I have condensed them from Woititz's original thirteen), here is an exercise I would like you to do in your journal. It is a diagnostic tool to help you understand how being an adult child is impacting on your daily life.

Where Are You an 'Adult Child'?

Write down your own list of all the characteristics and behaviours that I've explained that you feel apply to you (and any others that you are aware of that have not been discussed above). If you need to edit or tweak them a bit to make them more true to you, please go ahead. Now establish how these characteristics and behaviours relate to each of these areas of your life:

- ★ intimate relationships
- ★ friendships
- ★ family

- ★ work and career
- ★ financial stability
- ★ physical fitness and strength
- ★ creativity and personal development
- ★ health

In general, how is your life affected by these thoughts and beliefs? Write down examples or situations where this is most in evidence for you. Then try to identify actions you can take to alter your beliefs and responses in each of the eight areas.

2 ✳

Some Limiting Beliefs of Adult Children

The characteristics identified by Janet Woititz are generally accepted as key to understanding and changing adult child behaviour. My own work as a coach to many adult children has helped me to identify a whole host of limiting beliefs and unconscious behaviour patterns that are related to these characteristics.

Limiting beliefs are exactly what they sound like: unconscious thoughts that limit us. They generally evolve as a self-protection mechanism, and are almost without exception a response to an emotional or physical hurt experienced in childhood. When we encounter danger or disappointment in childhood, our survival instinct takes over and what I call our Survivor Self steps in to protect us from physical or emotional harm. Our survivor self makes sense of the world as we experience it at that moment and responds with a whole range of ideas and beliefs that are designed to keep us safe. The Survivor Self of someone who was consistently let down by unreliable parents or caregivers may start to believe that 'I can't rely on anyone else.' In the short term, this would probably be very effective in protecting against future disappointment but, as life progresses, this belief will start to limit the ability of the person who unconsciously believes it to form functional and effective relationships.

While they may be very apt and appropriate at the time of origination, Survivor Self beliefs and strategies have a habit of progressing from protecting to limiting. When they have passed their best-before date, it is time to identify them and decide if they are still protecting us, or if they have started to limit and restrict us.

There are some limiting beliefs that are pretty common and applicable to many adult children, but every person is different and has their own individual set of limiting beliefs and behaviours. Even siblings who grew up in the same family each have their own unique exposure to and experience of relationships and the world they live in.

The range of possible limiting beliefs is so wide and large it is not possible to present them all here. We will go through the main ones, the ones that I come across almost every day in my professional life. I hope that by sharing these with you, you will be able to identify your own personal limiting beliefs, along with recognising how they may have originated.

'If I were better, it would be better'

The most common and all-encompassing limiting belief is the one you've already heard me use a few times so far. It's the one I like to call 'If I were better, it would be better'. This can relate to anything in life – other people's unhappiness, bad relationships, toxic work environments, even the state of the world and the environment.

As we have discussed, part of a child's psychological development involves feeling as though they are the centre of the universe. From a very young age children believe that things happen because of or in response to their behaviour. When good things happen, it is because they are good and when bad things happen it must be because they are not good enough.
In the child's mind, they are responsible for the bad tempers, unhappinesses, frustrations, sadnesses, and disappointments of the adults who are raising them, and if they could just get it right, the grown-ups will be happy and will be able to love and care for the child in the way they crave. This is not helped if parents make statements such as 'You should have done better' or 'Why didn't you ...' or, like Helen's mother, 'It's your fault I am so unhappy.' Adult children often unconsciously believe that if they change and improve, then their environment will change and improve. So they try to be better. They lose weight,

have plastic surgery, try to be more loving, learn new skills, work harder, recycle more plastic, give more to charity ... all in an attempt to make themselves – and the situation – better.

Melanie is gorgeous. She is tall and slim and has waves of curly dark hair that frame her pretty face. She is clever, too, and has a great job in advertising. She is funny and gregarious and comes across as happy and successful. On the outside, she has it all together, but on the inside she is still the little girl who used to hide under the bed with her younger sister to escape their father's drink-fuelled violent rages.

'As soon as we would hear his car come through the gate, we would run and hide,' she confides. Melanie is married to a man surprisingly similar to her father in many respects. While he does not physically hurt her, the emotional abuse he inflicts on her is perhaps even more painful. Sometimes he does not come home at all – not bothering to hide the fact that he has spent the night with another woman. He constantly tells her how she could be improving herself; her looks, her accomplishments, even her thought processes. Not only does she have an unconscious and deeply held belief that if she were better, it would be better, she hears the message 'if you were better, it would be better' loud and clear every day.

Despite the fact that she gets seasick, Melanie has taken up scuba diving, because it's her husband's sport. She is going on a cooking course to try and learn new recipes that she can make for him when she gets home at seven o'clock at night. She reads books and magazines she's not interested in in the hope that she will be able to express an opinion that he'll approve of. The adult part of Melanie knows that it is not her that should be better, but him, but the scared child in her is just trying to avoid being beaten, by being as good and compliant as she can possibly be. Her inner child feels powerless to make choices, and she needs to dig deep to access the adult who can choose a different path.

'I am not good enough'

A close relative of 'If I were better, it would be better', the fear of not being good enough can result in a limiting belief that may be debilitating. For many adults who are driven to succeed and excel, this fear can be the driving force behind much of their innovation and achievement. What makes it different with adult children, however, is that it is not just a fear – it is a *conviction*.

Time and again, I work with clients who have this belief as their core issue. For people who are not adult children (and there *are* some) this thought is a fear which they may be driven to disprove by pushing themselves to achieve in many areas of their lives. But for the adult child, it is not so much a fear as, for them at least, a deeply held, irrefutable truth. It doesn't matter how well they do, how much they achieve, or how much they contribute. Many adult children continue to believe that they just aren't good enough. The difficulty, as is the case with all limiting beliefs, is that it is more often than not unconscious. It is an underlying subliminal conviction that motivates all their thoughts and actions.

When that belief is brought out into the open, it can be examined and thought through consciously and logically. It is relatively easy to disprove false beliefs when they are calmly and rationally thought through. The trick is to become conscious of them!

Roger is a lovely looking man – tall, dark and handsome with curly brown hair and big green eyes – and clever, compassionate and entertaining to boot. He is a great example of how the limiting belief 'I am not good enough' can immobilise the adult child, as opposed to spurring him on to greater success. Roger had parents who were physically present but emotionally absent.

'I remember my older sister sitting up all night to help me finish making my costume for the school play,' he told me at one of our earlier sessions. 'I can't remember where my parents were. I think they were around, but they didn't seem to care. Sometimes my father was so lovely and played such wonderful games with us, but mostly he didn't seem to be aware of our existence.'

Roger holds a very stressful and high powered job in a company that provides internet services to government. At best such an environment can be viewed as dynamic and innovative, and constantly changing, with technology that is advancing faster than the ice caps are melting. Unpredictable and not very consistent is another way of seeing it – just like the childhood that Roger had. Like so many adult children, Roger is drawn to work in organisations and environments that somehow reflect and recreate the chaotic and uncontaining experiences of his childhood. As a young boy he had not felt good enough – if he was good enough, then surely his father would have noticed him and been nice to him every day, rather than only very occasionally – and as a man this belief was limiting his ability to do his job well, and to enjoy his life.

His work felt like an emotional rollercoaster. Every now and then a project would be going really well and he would bask in the positive emotions of achievement and recognition, but then something in the broader environment would shift – some technical advance in the world of computers and the internet would take place, and necessitate a change to his plan – and leave him feeling devastated and useless. All Roger's fears about not being good enough would come up again: if he were good enough, he would have been able to anticipate every external development, every new program and project would be seamless and have no hitches, and his staff would never feel stressed, tired and anxious.

When a staff member made a costly mistake it was, at least according to Roger, Roger's fault. He was to blame for every gremlin that got into the complex and sensitive system they were developing, and the fact that the budgets that he was working with were increasingly affected by the global recession was clearly because he was not good enough and had nothing to do with external factors. Even the breakdown of a colleague's marriage was somehow because Roger was not good enough; he should have seen that the man in question was struggling, and insisted he go to marriage counselling. So he, Roger, is to blame for his colleague's imminent divorce.

Roger's struggle at work is made worse by another, equally debilitating belief: 'I **can't ask for help**.' Adult children who grew up in families where their parents or primary caregivers were not tuned in enough to offer help when it was needed, or able to provide help when it was asked for, develop a fiercely self-reliant streak which makes them very independent and resourceful. Sadly this self-reliance can also trap them in a situation that, because they have not created it, they cannot fix all on their own.

Roger is an adult child caught in an ever-changing and confusing environment, trying to make sense of it all on his own, attempting to pre-empt anything that may possibly go wrong by having all the answers, and in the end tasting bitter disappointment – in himself, of course – when things go wrong. Even then, it is hard for him to ask for help because of the fear that it will only confirm what he already knows; that he is not good enough.

'I don't deserve to have more than others'

'I don't deserve to have more than others' is a belief that is often prevalent in people who have managed to escape a troubled or challenging environment and create a better life for themselves. A kind of survivor guilt descends when they are confronted with evidence of those they left behind, the ones who haven't managed to do as well as they have. The guilt is not confined to friends or relatives; even when confronted with perfect strangers who have less, many adult children will feel a guilt about having more and being more fortunate.

There is a strong drive to respond by 'giving your toys away', which is what I call the compulsion for many adult children to share or give away their hard-won gains – not just their material possessions but also their time, skills, knowledge and often even friends and loved ones. In South Africa, where we are all confronted every day with evidence of people who are far worse off than we are, this limiting belief can start to feel overwhelming and crippling.

Lance and Lebo both illustrate this belief very well. Lance has built up an incredibly successful company over the last ten years. He trains up young professionals whom he then 'buys in' whenever he needs additional skills for a large job. In theory. In practice, Lance often feels so responsible for these young peoples' success that he outsources work to them that he would like to do himself, even when he could do with the extra income himself. Then he becomes resentful when the people he has developed start doing better financially than he's doing.

Lebo loves her work, lives in a beautiful home, is very happily married, and has happy and successful children. The only fly in the ointment is her constant guilt about having so much more than her twice-divorced single parent sister who can't hold down a job and drinks liberally and often. In an attempt to make her sister happier, Lebo tries to share her good fortune by buying her sister new clothes whenever she shops for herself, taking her sister and her children on holidays with her own family, and introducing her sister to all of her single male friends. The fact that none of these strategies helps to make her sister feel less resentful seems to escape Lebo's notice. Or, if she does notice, she ignores it, and keeps on hoping to persuade her sister to love her more by doing the equivalent of handing over her favourite doll.

'If I stand up for myself, I will be rejecting'

While the associated survivour self belief 'If I stand up for myself, I will be reject*ed*' is a relatively common fear among a wide range of people who have been socialised into doing what is expected of them rather than pleasing themselves, the fear of being reject*ing* is a serious issue for many adult children.

The idea of causing others to feel as bad as they have felt in their own lives is intolerable for adult children and can contribute to them agreeing to do things that they really do not want to do, or to not doing things that they really *do* want to do.

Delia was 'the clever one' in her family. Her sister and brother were constantly told how brilliant Delia was, and how she was going to go further in her studies than her siblings. At the time this made Delia feel deeply uncomfortable. She worried that her cleverness made her sister and brother feel less clever, which led to them feeling bad about themselves and possibly even resentful of her. So Delia learned compliance and the art of fading into the background from a very early age. Now in her forties, she has become aware of how she holds herself back at work, and never stands up for herself by drawing attention to her accomplishments or asking for promotions or raises. She realises that this is because she is protecting her colleagues from the feelings of inadequacy she fears they will feel in comparison to her brilliance.

'I can't ask for help' or 'I have to do everything by myself' or 'I can't rely on anyone else'

Adult children have got used to being self-sufficient, either to avoid the disappointment of being let down when help was not forthcoming, or because there was no one appropriate to ask for help from. For some adult children, there may be a slight undercurrent of victimhood or martyrdom but I believe that, for the most part, it just does not occur to them that there may be someone able or willing to lend a hand. It sometimes seems easier for the adult child to opt out of a course of action completely, rather than ask for help. Often, too, adult children struggle to delegate and end up suffering from burnout that comes from chronic work overload.

Despite displaying an almost pathological inability to ask for help, many adult children seethe with resentment towards their family, friends and co-workers for not offering to help; they shouldn't have to be told or asked.

Mary runs herself ragged at her job as a senior executive in a big organisation. She manages her immediate team of 30 and is indirectly responsible for a further 120 staff members. Having been the child her mother pinned all her hopes on – to the obvious anger of her father who used to verbally abuse her regularly and beat her on occasion – Mary is used to looking after other people and trying to keep them happy by being perfect. First she worked on being a perfect child, then a perfect student, then a perfect employee, and now she tries to be a perfect manager. She tries to do her own work, ensure that the 150 people she manages all do their work, and keep everybody happy, all without asking for help. She came to a session with me sunken-eyed and grey with exhaustion. I asked her if it was entirely necessary that she do all the work she was busy with herself, rather than delegating some of her responsibilities. 'Of course I should be delegating,' she said, 'but I feel bad asking them because they are all working so hard already.'

'What about asking your own manager for some help?' I suggest.

'I am not asking him for help!' Mary was horrified. 'He can see how hard we are all working and he doesn't care. He is the most unsupportive person in the whole organisation.'

'If I say no, I may never be asked again'

Like Roger and so many other adult children, Mary's struggle to ask for help is exacerbated by a deep and abiding belief that, despite all evidence to the contrary, she is not good enough at her job. This in turn is linked to the Survivour Self belief 'If I say no, I may never be asked again' (or may never be promoted or given an increase). Adult children are so happy to be noticed and paid attention to that they frequently find themselves saying yes to job offers, dates or 'opportunities' even if they don't want them, thereby finding themselves in relationships or careers that do not make them happy, but which they feel compelled to stay in rather than confront the fear of having nothing.

'It is my fault when someone dissapoints me'

One of the most debilitating beliefs that many adult children aren't even aware that they carry is 'It is my fault when someone disappoints me or something goes wrong'.

Many adult children assume responsibility for other people's bad behaviour. It is very difficult for adult children to stop making excuses for the people they love because for most of them this is something they have done from a very early age. If someone is unreliable and forgets to call when they said they would, it must be the adult child's fault for not being clear enough, or for being too pushy or too needy. Maybe they said something to upset that person and that's why they haven't called.

This was exactly what Angela's instinct was when her husband disappointed her by having an affair. She was sure she must have done something wrong to drive him into the arms of another woman. Maybe it was those extra two kilograms she put on with the baby and just could not get rid of. Or maybe it was because she wasn't interesting enough anymore. Or maybe she hadn't been making him nice enough lunches to take to work.

Rather than allowing herself to feel what would have been justified anger and betrayal, Angela slipped into the habit, developed in childhood, of imagining how she would like things to be, or remembering how things used to be. 'We were so happy when we first got together, we had the perfect relationship. All my friends were jealous of how well he treated me. Maybe if I help him get his promotion he will feel less insecure and remember how much he loves me.'

'It will get better' or 'It used to be better'

Seeing reality is often difficult for adult children. 'It **will get better**' or 'It **used to be better**' are fantasies that helped the child in a chaotic home survive an unhappy childhood that was far from good, and results in adults who often find it very hard to be present in the moment. As children they had no control over their environment and were unable to leave it, no matter how much they may have wished they could. The only way to tolerate situations that may have felt overwhelming was to remember good things that had happened in the past, or to retreat into a dream world and imagine and hope for how things might improve in the future.

When relationships turn sour, adult children tend to stay in them for much longer than they should, by remembering all the good things about the person and, like a child, by persuading themselves that that person will be good again. It is very hard for adult children with this trait to get over relationships that have ended, as there is a tendency to look at what was or what might have been rather than at what is.

'If I am not needed, I will be forgotten about'

Because so many children growing up in troubled families feel invisible, it is not uncommon for them to develop a need to be needed. The thinking is that if they are indispensable, they will not be forgotten about. Behaviours as adults that demonstrate this belief include taking on lots of responsibility at work, being all things to all people, never saying no to requests for their time and attention, and being very kind and considerate and caring friends who are always available and put their friends' and family's needs above their own. Nothing is too much trouble for an adult child if it means not being forgotten. Not only is this a recipe for burnout, it also may result in frequent over-involvement in other people's problems.

Janet personifies this limiting belief, and takes others–centredness to a new level. She finds it incredibly difficult to say no to anyone. Despite the fact that she has a demanding job and family life, she sits on more committees – residents' associations, school boards, fundraising committees, the 'fun' committee at work – than anyone can be expected to keep track of. She insists on being the one to fetch and carry her children to every extramural event, makes every dinner herself from scratch, and likes to feel indispensable at work and also in the lives of her brothers and their families. She is so busy making sure that everyone else needs her that she forgets to think about what she may need for herself. No wonder that this petite woman is beginning to look a little frayed around her pretty blonde edges.

Adult children are often particularly good in a crisis. In *The Adult Child of Alcoholics Syndrome*, Kritsberg talks about 'crisis-oriented living' and describes how being involved in drama and crisis can give the adult child a sense of being alive and useful, while providing a convenient deflection from their thoughts and feelings.

Being able to swoop in and save the day is manna from heaven for an adult child who needs to be needed.

'Don't tell me what to do'

Adult children often struggle with authority. While it is not strictly speaking a limiting belief, '**Don't tell me what to do**' is certainly an attitude that is held by many adult children, and which often does not serve them. After a lifetime of feeling as though they are making their own way in the world, with no one to rely on and no one to ask for help, many adult children feel deeply resentful of people who give them instructions or even well-meant advice. They may deliberately not follow suggestions or orders, which can make life very hard.

Patience marched into my office in a fit of righteous indignation. Normally a softly spoken and gently rounded woman, today she is all spiky irritation and hard edges. 'You are not going to believe what my idiot boss did to me today!' she announces with no small degree of relish. Were it not for the fact that for weeks I had heard numerous stories of her boss's lack of consideration, arrogance and all round idiocy, I may have been a bit more concerned. But the fact is, the boss's own foibles – and I am sure he was not an easy man – aside, Patience does not respond well to being told what to do, to being questioned on what she has already done, or to being second-guessed. Sometimes she can be her own worst enemy, because she is so quick to take offense that she often misses the occasional positive and constructive comments that her boss makes.

Survivor Self beliefs start out feeling like the truth when we are children and need to protect ourselves from pain and disappointment but, if unexamined and left to fester, they rapidly become lies. We need to identify them, examine them critically and, if they are not serving us anymore, we need to discard them so that we can move forward happily and healthily.

Tell Yourself the Truth

Using the insights you gained from completing the exercise in the previous chapter, write a list of some of your own limiting beliefs. Now, draw a line down the middle of a fresh page in your journal and write all of the limiting beliefs you have identified for yourself in the left-hand column. Use the right-hand column to record as many reasons as you can think of (at least three, please) that show how that belief may not be true. Your page will probably look a little like this:

My limiting belief or behaviour	Why it is not true
If I am not needed, I will be forgotten about	My friends do not need me and they don't forget about me
	I ran into an acquaintance I had met only once before and they remembered me and asked how my job was going
If I say no, I may never be asked again	I said no to an invitation to a movie last week and my friend asked me again this week
	I turned down a job offer and got another one

With your new knowledge that these limiting beliefs are not true, I suggest you revisit your eight life areas and identify at least one small behavioural change you can make in each of them.

3

Adult children struggle to feel like adults

The numerous and varied limiting beliefs and behaviours that accompany adult children through their lives are aided and abetted by the way adult children see themselves in relation to those around them – at work, at play, in love and everywhere else. We can understand this process a little better through a brief examination of communication processes.

Eric Berne's theory of how people communicate, Transactional Analysis (TA) helps us to understand the way we speak and how we behave in relation to others. Despite the way it sounds, TA is not concerned with examining your bank statements, but is rather a very clever and helpful model that explains the way people relate to each other. You can read more about it in Berne's book *Games People Play*, which provides an in-depth and comprehensive discussion of his ideas.

I believe that Berne's ideas and model of TA perfectly describe and explain how communication processes work, and why they can so easily go awry. I have taken a few key principles from this extremely complex and comprehensive field of psychology and distilled and simplified them into what I hope is an easy way to understand communication and conflict.

Essentially, Berne explains that we all have three ego states from which we operate: Parent, Adult and Child. This is how I describe the ego states to my clients:

When we are in our ***Parent ego state***, we are either being Critical (or Controlling) or Nurturing. Our Critical Parent is that part of us that comes out when we feel a need to be in control. It is our bossy side that says things like 'Under no circumstances should you…' or 'You must…' or 'You have to…' or 'What were you thinking?' or 'How could you?'. This is the part of us that (literally or figuratively) waves our index finger around and points out what we think other people should be doing, and how they should be doing it. By contrast, when we are in our Nurturing Parent ego state, we feel as though we need to look after others, to help them and to make things better for them.

When we are in our ***Adult ego state***, we are feeling calm, rational and empowered. We are able to respond appropriately to the situation we find ourselves in – and from a state of equality and competence, rather than reacting critically or fearfully.

The **Child ego state** is the vulnerable, anxious, defensive and sometimes truculent part of us. It's the part of us that responds from a child-like place of play, fear or rebellion. There are three ways that the Child ego state manifests itself. When we are in our Natural Child state, we are able to play and laugh and have fun in a carefree manner. This is not generally a state that is familiar to most adult children, but it is one that we can access when we are playing with our own children or spending time with friends in a relaxed and playful environment like a girls' night out or going to a rugby game with mates. We find ourselves in our Frightened Child when we feel very scared of being hurt (either physically or emotionally), being rejected, or being shamed. It is the part of us that takes over and expects the worst when we are called into our boss's office, or fears that we are about to be broken up with when we receive a text that says, 'We need to talk.' This state can leave us feeling like a victim that is somewhat put-upon and in need of looking after or rescuing. The Rebellious Child ego state is the part of us that says (or thinks), 'You are not the boss of me!' It's the part that doesn't like to be told what to do. Being in this state when we are angry or upset can result in passive/aggressive behaviour, sulking or throwing of tantrums. The Child ego state is not an empowering state to be in.

Berne describes interactions as taking place between an initiator and a responder. The state that the initiator comes from influences the state of the responder. We respond automatically and unconsciously to the ego state of the person who has initiated the interaction. A Parent ego state elicits a response from Child, a Child state elicits a response from Parent (or Child, which is often what happens in our intimate relationships when we get into a 'You started it' – 'No, you started it' squabble). An Adult ego state will get a response from an Adult ego state.

The real power of TA is in the understanding that in all of our interactions, we react not to the words that are being used, but to the way the person who is saying those words is feeling when they utter them. Take complaining about something that has upset you, for example. You can consciously choose to use words that are rational and appropriate and faultlessly logical, but if you are saying them from your Parent state, the people you are speaking to will be either too terrified or too truculent to respond satisfactorily.

Often, too, we are not even exchanging words, yet our ego states are communicating with each other. Think about what happens in a queue of traffic when someone tries to push in front of you. I don't know about you, but unless I am being extremely careful and mindful about my response, I will respond to that Rebellious Child behaviour with either my own Rebellious Child or my Critical Parent. I will try to push them back out, or I will launch into a Critical Parent tirade against them in my car: 'Who do you think you are? What makes you think you are more important than the rest of us?' I will fume to myself. All this without even being in the same physical space as the other person, let alone exchanging actual words with them.

When we understand Transactional Analysis and the power of the ego states, we start to understand how and why we respond to the people around us the way we do.

When Melanie's husband behaved like her father and told her that she was not interesting enough, she responded to him from the Frightened Child state, trying harder and reading more in an attempt to gain his approval and avoid being hurt.

When Helen's mother behaved like a Rebellious Child, lying on her bed and having a tantrum, seven-year-old Helen was forced into a Nurturing Parent state, comforting her mother and bringing her tea to make her feel better.

The optimal ego state to be in and communicate from is Adult, but this often goes awry, as anyone who has spent any time in rush hour traffic will know. One of my favourite games that I play is to identify the Adult, Parent and Child ego state that I see in the interactions that go on around me. Try it yourself. You will be amazed at how few Adult to Adult interactions take place.

Staying in the Adult state when in a situation of stress or pressure of any kind is hard for everyone, but communicating with others from a mature Adult perspective can be particularly hard for adult children. They often did not have very reliable role models to show them what being Adult looks and sounds like, and they are very used to slipping into Parent or Child states. In a situation that has the potential to make the adult child feel anxious and unworthy, they may adopt the Child role, unconsciously giving up their power by allowing the other person or people to step into the Parental one. Or they may step into Parent, not trusting that anyone else will take control and becoming bossy and controlling, or sweetly smothering the people around them.

Does any of this sound familiar?

The truly fascinating thing about this model is how the communication flows in a straight line between two people. Unless the line is moved by one of the people in the transaction, the communication flow will continue between Parent and Child, Parent and Parent, Child and Child and, occasionally, Adult and Adult. It is possible to shift that communication line, however. By consciously choosing to respond from an Adult state, you move the person you are communicating with into Adult too. Even if the person you are communicating with starts off an interaction from the Parent or Child states, by deliberately responding from an Adult state, you can 'force' them (gently) into Adult themselves.

My favourite and most frequently used tool is the one below. I assign it to all of my clients as homework and the results are astounding. By subtly shifting the way they relate to their partners, colleagues, even their parents, they change the whole dynamic of many of their relationships without having to hold a council of war discussion about how they want things to change. They show, rather than tell, how they want things to be different.

Act Like a Grown-Up

Spend some time thinking about occasions when you have acted from each of the Parent, Adult or Child states. What kinds of situations in your personal and professional lives cause you to become Parental or Childlike?

Even though the ultimate way of relating is Adult to Adult, many adult children struggle to do this because we have not witnessed it enough in our own lives to know how it is done. I encourage you to 'take a step back' when you are in a situation that is making you anxious or fearful, and try to evaluate if you are in your Parent, Adult or Child state. If you are not in an Adult state, try to step into an Adult frame of mind. To help you with this, identify an Adult role model – someone you think is mature and sets an excellent example of behaving as an Adult at all times (it could be Nelson Mandela, or Barack Obama, or your granny – anyone you admire) and ask yourself: What would they do? How would they respond and act?

Then try to behave the way you think they would.

4

Adult Children Can Change How They Are

If you struggle to relax, experience work and/or relationships as battlefields, and live with anxiety, please be reassured that this is not because there is something wrong with you – it is because there is something 'wrong' with the way you grew up.

When I first started with this adult child work, I had a vague, mostly unconscious idea that I was coming across so many adult children because of South Africa's very particular and long history of segregation and political upheaval, which I imagined to be exacerbated by our enormously high HIV infection rate. 'Seperate development' and migrant labour combined to separate children from their parents and the HIV epidemic of the 90s resulted in huge numbers of child-headed households. Too many South African children grew up apart from their parents. But then I started working with clients from other countries and I realised that the factors that I considered particular to South Africa are present wherever you go.

All over the world, families have been, are still, and will continue to be affected by challenges to the health and happiness of their individual and collective members. Some of these challenges will be internal to the family – parents who are unpredictable or absent due to depression, addiction, illness, violence, etc – while circumstances and events that are *external* to the family can have just as devastating a consequence on the growing child. There are countless families and children who are affected by both man-made and natural disasters.

Wars wreak havoc not only with the families in the countries in which the war is taking place, but also with the families who have fathers, sons, brothers (and increasingly, mothers, daughters and sisters) who are sent into combat in another country. Political systems or events that demand that people be separated for any length of time can also result in fragmented families and insecure childhoods. Think of all those children who have been separated from one or both of their parents by genocides, ethnic cleansing programmes, and even the construction of seemingly randomly selected barriers between and within countries. I know a story of a young German girl who set off on her bicycle one morning to visit an aunt on the other side of town, and could not go back home to her parents because during the time she was away from home the Berlin Wall was erected.

And then of course there are natural disasters. Earthquakes, volcanoes, tsunamis or hurricanes – these unpreventable events will change the life trajectory of all who are affected by them almost instantly. Not to mention the family crises that are brought about by a combination of environmental and human factors: famine and AIDS being just two.

Whatever force may have impacted your family, be it internal, external, or a combination of the two, it is possible to reverse the damage, and to learn new ways of being in the world.

Lindi is a gorgeous young woman, clever, educated, articulate, bubbly and vivacious. I (and most people, I am sure) can see that she is extremely good at her job in public relations, even though she can't. Every second week, she comes to my office, sits opposite me and talks about her struggle to feel good enough in all areas of her life. I can always tell what kind of session we are going to have as she walks up the path to my office door. She has an extremely expressive face and her body is a canvas for her moods. Her shoes, though, are the real give-away: funky heels show that she is in a good space – she is self-confident and sassy. When she is in dark, nondescript shoes I know that we are in for an hour of self-recrimination and assessments of her own performance so harsh they make her sound like a crotchety old woman for whom nothing is ever good enough. A crotchety old woman, interestingly enough, who bears a striking resemblance to the grumpy grandmother who raised Lindi.

Now in her early thirties, Lindi still bears the emotional scars of being raised by a woman who belonged to the 'spare the rod and spoil the child' school of thought. It was bad enough that her parents had sent her away to be brought up by someone else, but that that someone else was cross, exhausted and volatile, made Lindi's childhood one that was lonely and emotionally sterile at best, and fraught with emotional and physical fear at worst.

With the benefit of hindsight, and as an adult, Lindi is able to see and understand that her parents were doing the best they could for their daughter, and that her grandmother was old and tired out from raising one set of children already. But as a child Lindi had felt the full extent of the fear of having been sent away because she was not good enough, and then of being continually shouted at and beaten because she was still not good enough. Somewhere along the line, the little girl developed a belief that if she was not so bad, then the situation would improve.

There it is again. 'If I were better, it would be better' – the limiting belief that is shared by so many adult children. The unconscious thoughts that give rise to this belief are always more or less the same: if I were better behaved/cleverer/prettier/stronger/braver, these bad things would not be happening.

To say that Lindi was afflicted with this limiting belief is about as accurate as saying that it is hot on the surface of the sun. She was so deeply affected by this belief that it infiltrated every area of her life. When colleagues did not follow through and deliver on what they were responsible for, Lindi not only picked up the slack and did their work for them, she also felt guilty about upsetting them, and worried that she was not doing a good enough job – at her own job *and* theirs.

When the man she had been hoping to marry started cheating on her, Lindi felt it must be her fault – if she had done something differently, he would never have strayed. Maybe if she hadn't been doing so well at work, and hadn't got that latest promotion ... Or maybe if she had spent more time cooking supper for him and ironing his shirts ... Lindi's fear of not being good enough at work translated into a fear about being too good at work for her boyfriend to love her. The unconscious belief 'If I were better, it would be better' was creating a lose-lose situation for her, just as it does for so many of the adult children I see in my practice.

Because so many adult children live their lives in a state of responsive reaction rather than planning proactively what they would like for themselves, they are constantly feeling that they are somehow to blame when things go wrong – for other people as well as for themselves – and responsible for making it better.

It took some time for Lindi to understand that her fear of not being good enough, and her unconscious urge to make herself better, were the cause of most of her anxiety and discomfort. When she was able to understand that she was not the problem she allowed herself to assess whether the work she was doing, or the man she was dating, were good enough for her, rather than if she were good enough for them. The day she marched up my path in leopard print stilettos, swinging her hips and beaming a dimpled smile that could light up a city, I knew Lindi and I would not be working together much longer. She settled herself on the couch in a cloud of joy and announced: 'I need to leave my job. I am too good for them.'

Many children are born into societies that are unstable and scary, and parents who are able to often choose to send their children to a place they regard as safer and better able to provide stability and opportunity for them. Think of all those children who were sent into the country to escape the bombing of London during World War Two, and the children who are sent to schools or universities in other countries for a 'better' education today.

Being sent away from their parents is devastating and confusing for any child. The additional worry for the safety of the parents, combined with the confusion arising from being in an unfamiliar environment, make it almost impossible to not develop adult child characteristics.

Bongi's father was very involved in politics throughout her childhood. She was sent to boarding school from a young age, both so that she would be exposed to a far better education than she would have had at a township day school at home, and also because, with her safely away from the political turmoil that they were in the midst of, her parents could concentrate on their political activities and give them the attention they needed.

A sensitive child, Bongi would probably have struggled at boarding school even if she hadn't had the constant worry that she might never see her beloved father again. Now a sensitive adult, she is very successful at a job she hates at a place where she feels different and struggles to feel liked and accepted by her colleagues, subordinates, peers and managers alike. Just as she felt different at boarding school, she now feels different at work. Even though she is talented, intelligent and extremely competent, she feels anxious all the time that she is in her office. All she really wants to do is draw and paint and create art that honours the memory of her much-missed late father. But Bongi struggles to give herself permission to leave the situation that she hates, and exchange it for an environment that is more comfortable and reflective of who she really is.

Bongi reached the point of no return when she decided that in order to feel liked and accepted she needed to like and accept herself. By allowing herself to understand why she is the way she is, and to look at how she wanted to change *how* she is in the world, she took up painting, enrolled in a pilates-instructor training programme, and started to write a book. She still didn't love her job, but she found she was getting on better with colleagues and feeling less lonely at work. At our last session together she was planning an overseas study tour – and her resignation.

The key change for Bongi was realising that she had choice. Too frequently, as adults, adult children do not recognise that they have choice now, because they didn't have one then.

Sometimes, we have no choice over what happens to us. The

world can be a very unsafe place and the death of parents is a sad reality for far too many children.

Isaac's mother died when he was five and he and his younger brother lived with their father until Isaac was nine years old, when his father also died, leaving Isaac feeling alone and scared and responsible not only for himself, but for his younger brother as well. For the next few years Isaac and his brother stayed first with their grandmother until she passed away, and then with a succession of relatives, all of whom were struggling to make ends meet and not managing to hide the stress of feeding and clothing two additional children.

'Moving from one relative to another, coupled with arguments as our aunts used to fight with their husbands about us, really made me feel guilty,' Isaac says. The two little boys had to walk long distances to school, more often than not on empty stomachs, and after he got home from school in the afternoon, Isaac sold firewood to neighbours in the townships to make money for himself and his brother, so as not to feel such a burden on his relatives.

Now very happily married, a proud father and well-respected team leader at work, Isaac is still a very anxious and nervous man. His core fear is 'If I am not good enough, I will be sent away.' This limiting belief, so ever-present in his childhood, is hampering his performance at work and causing all sorts of health problems from the constant pressure he puts himself under as a husband, father, brother and uncle. Isaac needed to learn that, not only is it not possible to be perfect all the time, it is also not desirable. When he came to the realisation that he could ask for help at work and at home, and that people were only too happy to oblige, and to be given an opportunity to give back a little to the man who gives so much, Isaac started to feel less anxious and to be more effective and more relaxed and happy.

The world is a very different place now than it was even a couple of decades ago. Better education, political change, rapid developments and technological advances have made access to education possible for many people whose parents did not have the same opportunities. Adult children who find themselves spoilt for choice in terms of their life and career paths have a particular challenge – that of allowing themselves to do and be what they choose, rather than what is offered to them.

Remember Zanele, who would disrobe on the front doorstep so as not to take her work home with her? During our first and only session, she revealed that despite being a director at her accounting firm, what she had dreamed of being since she was a child was a teacher. But for Zanele, and many others like her, whose parents did not have the opportunity to be high-powered executives, the pressure to make up for her parents' lack of choice, made her feel that she did not have choice herself. To be a teacher was unthinkable – she needed to realise her father's stunted ambitions for himself.

Too much choice also proved to be a burden for Mpume who had been promoted three times in 18 months, her salary had quadrupled in two years and she was in a position that she had neither the experience nor the maturity to manage properly. She was miserable. She was out of her depth and she knew it, but she felt that she had no options. With a large extended family that was expecting her to help them financially, a bond on a new home and car to finance, she found herself, at the age of 28, in a position that was overwhelming for her. Her well developed sense of responsibility and inability to say no left Mpume stuck in a place that reinforced all her fears about not being good enough, and needing to be better to make the situation better. Luckily she realised what was going on and made a decision to stay where she was until she had consolidated her skills and experience, and she made a commitment to herself to not speak to any more head-hunters for at least two years. The opportunities would still be there when she was ready, even if she said no to some now.

At the time of writing this book the world has just experienced one of the worst recessions of our time. Literally millions of jobs have been lost and countless families have been affected by a drop in income.

Aaron is a bright, beautiful young man. He loves his job, the first he has ever had, and has got steadily better at it over the year that he has been employed. He has a great relationship with his colleagues and he genuinely enjoys the content of his work. But now he is looking around for another job because he feels that he needs to earn more money in order to help support his extended family. As one of the few people in his family to have a job, and because he is an extremely dutiful son, he adds his own unreasonable expectations to the frequent requests for financial support that he receives from his siblings, cousins and aunts. Aaron is all of 23 years old.

It is a very complex and difficult situation, and one in which so many people find themselves. How do you put your own needs above others, when all around you is evidence of how much better off you are? It has taken some time and a great deal of effort, but Aaron has eventually been able to take the pressure to find another job off himself, and has allowed himself to stay in the one he already has. There he will be able to grow and develop, take advantage of the bursary scheme the company he works for offers and study further, and gain sufficient experience and knowledge to either be promoted internally, or to find a better position in another company when the time is right. Aaron is not the only one who feels relieved by this decision: his mother, when told about it, was over the moon that her son was staying in a place that was so obviously good for him.

Limiting Expectations

I believe that adult children are particularly prone to 'imposing' and responding to what I call 'limiting expectations' in the workplace. You'll have become very familiar by now with the definition of a limiting belief, an (usually) unconscious belief that we have about ourselves that limits us or holds us back from being the best that we can be.

Often, too, we have unconscious beliefs about what we can expect of other people and their capabilities or behaviours – and of ourselves and our own abilities. These are 'limiting expectations'. Limiting expectations play themselves out just as powerfully as limiting beliefs. When we unconsciously treat people the way we expect them to be, and they in turn unconsciously meet that expectation by behaving in that way. We also unconsciously meet others' unspoken expectations.

Say for example the first time we meet a new colleague she is flustered and shy and not very articulate. She may be all these things because the boss has asked her to do something that has taken longer than expected and she was worried about being late for the meeting. We don't have all that background information. All we have is how she appears to us the first time we meet her. So we treat her like someone who is flustered, shy and inarticulate, and – guess what? She will probably live up to this expectation by *being* flustered, shy and inarticulate whenever she's around us!

Similarly, if we are that new employee being treated as someone who is unconfident and unable to express herself clearly, we can unconsciously become that person. Who hasn't turned into the 'difficult', 'shy' or 'stupid' child when visiting parents, no matter how well behaved, confident and clever you may be in another setting?

The expectations we have of and for ourselves can also be limiting. Time and time again, I work with clients who bewail the fact that they haven't managed to get promoted, get married or become financially free. When we are able to explore their stories a bit more, it becomes obvious that it is the unconscious expectations they have of and for themselves that are holding them back from getting where they want to be. It is very hard for someone who believes they will never amount to much, to ever amount to much. Or for someone who doesn't believe that they will ever find romantic happiness to be romantically happy.

Limiting Expectations You Have Known

Now it's your turn to identify some of the limiting expectations that you might have experienced. Take a clean sheet of paper and draw a column down the middle. Title the left-hand column 'Limiting Expectations that others have about me' and the right-hand column 'Limiting Expectations that I have had about others'. Think about how you may have met the limiting expectations others have had about you. And how the people you have had limiting expectations about have met these expectations.

Often, interestingly, the limiting expectations we have about others, are the same ones we feel have been imposed on us.

Whether the imperfection of a childhood was a result of disease that originated within the family or from the outside, the results are similar. Having an in depth knowledge and understanding of the background and family dynamics that produced an adult child is less important than understanding the effects on the adult child now. The context that created an adult child, is not the issue as much as the manifestation of the characteristics, behaviours and limiting beliefs are. When we understand that our foibles and anxieties are common to other adult children, we can see that they are part of a syndrome that has very little to do with each individual.

It is possible to change, and it is less difficult than you may fear. One step at a time, you can improve your quality of life by making different choices and responding in different ways. When we understand why we are the way we are, then we can start to make changes to how we are. Not *who* we are, but *how* we are.

Ten Steps to Change

Make a list of ten small — and I really mean small — changes you can make to improve your life. If, for example, you struggle to ask for help, think of something small you can ask someone to help you with. If you need to be needed, try turning your cellphone off for a couple of hours and have a relaxing bath or read a book you are looking forward to reading. Do at least one of these small things EVERY DAY. Then write about how it makes you feel in your journal.

5

Adult Children In and Out of Love

All Stacey wanted was for her boyfriend to ask her to marry him. Throughout many years of their relationship, she worked hard at being the kind of partner he wanted, and even harder at trying to get him to be the kind of partner *she* wanted. She came into the room for our fifth session together and told me that he had popped the question the previous night. She was engaged at last. After a few moments of making what I thought to be the requisite noises of excitement and victory I noticed that Stacey was not looking like your typical recently affianced and soon to be blushing bride. I asked her outright what the problem was.

'Well,' she said, 'I am not sure anymore that I really want to marry him.'

While I liked to think that the hard work Stacey had been putting into understanding what being an adult child meant had helped her to see that she had possibly been putting up with second best all these years, and that that was why she was having doubts, I don't think this was the case. I feared that the sheer enormity of realising that she was committing to a lifetime of intimacy and trust may have had more to do with it.

Actually, it was both of these things, and as we worked together over the coming months Stacey was able to see where she had been making excuses – for herself and her fiancé – and overlooking behaviours and patterns that were negative for her and for the relationship. She was also able to learn to trust herself more and, in so doing, trust that the partnership would not destroy or trap her. She started to feel and act like an adult, and so did he.

As we know, adult children struggle to feel grown up in many areas of their lives, and their intimate relationships can be an arena of great distress and dissatisfaction. With an understanding of the adult child syndrome and its accompanying limiting beliefs and behaviours, it is easy to understand why allowing themselves to love may be a problem.

Two of Janet Woititz's characteristics of adult children directly relate to adult children and love:

* Adult children have trouble with intimate relationships and
* Adult children are intensely loyal even when it is obvious that their loyalty may be misplaced

Not all adult children struggle with relationships to the same degree. There are many adult children who are in stable and loving relationships. But for many others their experience of relationships in a chaotic childhood lays the foundation for their intimate relationships later in life.

What is a Healthy Relationship?

Many adult children have neither witnessed nor experienced a healthy relationship in their childhood, so they may struggle to imagine what this might look and feel like. A healthy relationship is one which allows and encourages both partners to grow, both as individuals and together as a couple. Each partner should feel that they can be themselves while also being part of a partnership that allows for give and take.

An intimate love relationship allows each partner to offer and to receive validation, understanding and a sense of being valued intellectually, emotionally and physically. The more each partner is able and willing to share, the greater the degree of intimacy between them. In this case intimacy does not only refer to the sexual side of a relationship, although this is certainly an aspect. Intimacy is about emotional, physical, intellectual and – often – material sharing and allowing the other person in.

People in healthy relationships allow another person be there for them; they ask for help and they are able to receive it. They accept their partners for who they are instead of trying to change them into who they would like them to be. Similarly, people in healthy relationships allow themselves to be who they are. They don't try to change into who they think their partners want them to be. There is an acceptance of each other. A healthy relationship frees the partners to be themselves.

This can be an unfamiliar experience for adult children, particularly when they struggle to allow themselves that freedom of self-acceptance.

Find a Healthy Relationship Role Model

Adult children often struggle to imagine being in a healthy relationship. Identify a relationship that you admire and think is a good, healthy one. Start with people you know or, if you can't think of a healthy relationship you have witnessed in action yourself, think of an example from a book or a movie.

How do the partners in this relationship communicate with each other? Using the Transactional Analysis model, ask yourself how they communicate. Is it primarily from the Parent, Adult or Child states.

What do you particularly admire about how they are with each other? Write your thoughts and observations down in your journal.

Who Do You Love?

Growing up, many adult children's experience of relationships may well have been that of inconsistency and confusion. If you have spent your childhood watching your parents' difficult relationship and experiencing your own troubled relationship with one or both of them, you may experience discomfort in the intimate relationships you form later on. As a child your experience of love may have been a confusing mixture of 'I love you', 'I need you', 'You are not good enough', 'Go away', 'It's your fault I'm so unhappy', and many other contradictory messages. This may understandably result in a deep-seated feeling of ambivalence towards relationships in general and individual partnerships in particular. It is relatively easy to understand why grown-ups who received mixed messages about their lovability – and the experience of love – in childhood may be drawn to potential partners who are inconsistent and unreliable. It is what feels familiar because of their early conditioning.

It is not surprising, then, that adult children are often drawn to lovers who mirror their childhood experience. When adult children *do* find someone who is consistent and reliable, it may be so unfamiliar to them that it feels uncomfortable.

It is often 'safer' for adult children to get involved with people who are unavailable, dangerous, unreliable, or unsuitable because they have a built-in protection against deep and lasting intimacy with these types of people. Also, the challenge of trying to win the love and undivided attention of an erratic, unreliable and/or sometimes rejecting person is often an unconscious repetition of the adult child's childhood challenge. For those adult children who thrive in crisis situations, there may also be an unconscious desire to be in a difficult or dramatic relationship because of the powerful stimulation that comes with these relationships.

Bella had recently broken up with her live-in boyfriend. Well, she had not so much broken up with him as thrown him out of her house – where he had been living rent free for two years – when she caught him cheating on her with his ex-wife. She was distraught and full of self-doubt. Maybe she'd been too harsh on him, maybe she'd driven him to it, maybe it was just a once-off and she had overreacted. And a lot more of the same 'If I were better, it would be better' self-talk. When it became clear he was not coming back, Bella convinced herself she was ready to move on and she started looking around for the next boyfriend.

There followed a succession of men upon whom Bella acted out her relationship pattern. She would choose someone inappropriate and/or unavailable, try to persuade them to change, try to change herself, ignore their obvious flaws, feel inadequate and not good enough because she couldn't change them, then finally give up and hibernate for a while.

In the first few months she came to me for coaching she dated a drug addict to whom she lent loads of money and had to bail out of jail at least once, a married man, and her ex-boyfriend who was now cheating on his ex-wife-now-current-girlfriend with Bella. She also developed a hopeless crush on a work colleague who was not only fifteen years younger than her, but also from a totally different religion, culture and context.

As Bella started to become aware of her patterns and to feel better about herself, she started to feel more Adult and less like the Parent. She also began to realise that she had no control over her partners' behaviour. She did, however, have control over *how* she was with her partners, or *if* she was with them. In the end she dumped them all and began to concentrate on making herself happy. And guess what – as soon as she started to allow herself to see and act the truth she started to notice the very nice, honest, reliable, dependable, gentle, kind man who had been hovering on the periphery of her social circle for years, and she experienced the first healthy and happy relationship she had ever had with a man.

Adult children constantly overlook the obvious inappropriateness of a possible partner. They make excuses for them and they try to change them into the partner they would like them to be. Why is the idea of changing someone who is unhappy or unhealthy into the perfect partner so appealing to so many adult children? It probably has a lot do with the denial that is such a strong form of self-sabotage for so many adult children (and we'll get to later) but it is also, I suspect, the thrill of the chase.

A need to control and to be in control of another person's behaviour stems from a deep need to create a sense of safety for the self – hence the desire to change a person and make him or her into what we believe is the perfect partner. Denial manifests in the adult child either through not noticing the partner's bad or unreliable behaviour, or by ignoring the warning signs. When the signs become reality, what does the adult child do? We make excuses for bad behaviour. Whatever it is they've done to demonstrate their unreliability the adult child will find a way to explain and excuse it. The irony is that the harder we try to control others, the less we are able to, and the harder it becomes to stop.

We all have our own conscious and unconscious expectations that colour the way we see and experience our world. Just as wearing sunglasses changes the shades and intensity of what we see, our expectations impact on our experience. We may don a pair of green-tinted lenses at work, and never feel that we get enough attention and praise, no matter how hard we try. In relation to love, adult children often have rose-tinted lenses which render them unable to see their partner in anything but the best light, while they see themselves through a different coloured lens – let's say yellow – which highlight the parts of themselves they do not think are good enough and they think they need to change.

These lenses have an enormous impact on the kinds of relationships adult children unconsciously seek out. If the lenses through which you view relationships in general are dark and grey, then miserable and dreary relationships will feel like the norm for you. They will be what you expect and – often – what you create.

What are the stories you tell yourself and others about relationships in general, and your own relationships in particular? Are you a fairytale ending person, convinced that love conquers all and as soon as your white knight (or Lady) arrives to rescue you and carry you off in his or her white convertible, all your troubles will be over? Or are you a cynic who believes that all relationships are doomed and a one-way ticket to financial and emotional bankruptcy?

How you think about love and relationships, and the stories you tell yourself and others, has an impact on how you experience love and relationships. How do you think your story plays out in your relationships?

If it hasn't been working for you, can you come up with a story that serves you better?

How Do You Love?

It can be quite a challenge to be in a relationship if you're an adult child. As if the general characteristics, behaviours and limiting beliefs that are common to many adult children aren't enough, there are some additional insecurities that are specific to the arena of relationships.

Relationships are one of the areas in our lives where we feel most vulnerable. All of our deepest fears and insecurities emerge in relationships. Because so many adult children received little real nurturing as children, there may be a deep-seated ambivalence about relationships. There is often an almost desperate need to become involved, but at the same time a terror of being in a relationship. Although they want to meet someone, they are fearful of giving up their independence. They themselves want to get to know everything about the person they are dating or involved with, but they get uncomfortable if their partner comes too close.

Adult children sometimes love too much or not at all – or swing between these two extremes. Not allowing themselves to love at all manifests in a continued emotional detachment, an ability to never quite reach a level of intimacy and trust with another person that would put them in emotional danger. There may be a sustained thought that they may in fact be better off on their own. In this way they are entirely in control of their emotions and never have to worry about being vulnerable or abandoned. If they do get involved in a relationship, they may be the first to withdraw as soon as they start to feel invested and the fear of being rejected raises its head.

Barry has not had a satisfying relationship since his wife of twelve years moved out sixteen years ago. Like his mother, his ex-wife was a functional alcoholic and he hadn't realised (or perhaps he had overlooked) the extent of her alcohol dependency until their second child started school. Their relationship limped on for a further five years, until her drinking got so extreme that Barry gave her an ultimatum. She moved out, leaving a devastated Barry to raise two traumatised children on his own. After more than twelve years of being so in love with his wife that he would not allow himself to see the truth of her destructive behaviour, Barry was a deeply wounded man. He no longer trusts himself or any woman he meets, to not hurt him again. He is a very attractive man, and has a lot going for him. Many women make it clear that they would like to pursue a relationship with him, but for Barry it is just too scary, and he very seldom goes on a third or fourth date with anyone. He is, in his own words, 'too scared to let anyone in again'. The role of doting father is much easier for him, and this is the one into which he puts all of his energy.

At the other end of the spectrum are those adult children who, because of their ability to remain intensely loyal, stay in relationships that are bad for them for much longer than they should. Sometimes they never leave. They manage this by losing themselves in the relationship and making everything all about the other person. They make excuses for bad behaviour (just like they did with their parents) and always look for the good in their partner. Remember Melanie, who would have turned herself inside out to make her husband happy? Just like her these adult children focus on who the person they are with *could* be rather than who that person really is. They take what attention they can get from their partner and put up with leftovers and scraps.

When it comes to themselves adult children, despite being generally very intuitive and tuned into the people around them, often override their intuition and ignore the warnings they receive about the unsuitability of certain partners. Instead, they set about trying to change themselves into who they think their partner wants them to be, or change their partner into who they want them to be – in both instances hoping to love them into submission.

Perhaps the most unsettling driver of adult children and love relationships is the need for excitement. This is related to the 'crisis-oriented living' that Kritsberg talks about. Feelings of drama and exhilaration can make adult children feel alive and useful, while at the same time giving them an excuse to not look at their own feelings and behaviour. The need for excitement can manifest in two ways: being in primary relationship(s) with people who are dangerous and unpredictable or who are themselves in crisis (for example, they could be unhappily married, or sick, or addicts or people in trouble with the law); or having affairs in order to add a sense of danger and excitement to what may otherwise feel like a stable and, therefore scary, relationship.

Kevin is dynamic and sociable and energises whatever room he is in. Creative and dynamic, he is at the top of his game at work and has a very happy home life with a loving wife and three beautiful children. In his early forties, he has reached a place that is so stable, so safe and so containing that it far exceeds what he imagined for himself when he was a child. Raised by a chronically depressed single parent mother who had a succession of boyfriends – some more suitable than others – Kevin's home life now is vastly different to what he grew familiar with in childhood, and it is terrifying the living daylights out of him.

'I feel bored,' he tells me at our first session. 'I think I need to shake things up a bit at work.' And shake them up he does – but not at work.

'I've met someone! Candy is perfect. She is my soulmate,' he announces within weeks.

'I thought your wife was your soulmate?' I ask, somewhat hesitantly.

'Well, she is of course, but this woman is my *real* soulmate. She is clever and funny, warm and wise and sexy as anything. She understands me. I have to be with her.'

Mercifully, Kevin was already in coaching and working on understanding what being an adult child means, so instead of rushing off to be with his new soulmate, he was able stay in his marriage and identify that it was his unconscious need for change, drama and excitement rather than his need for Candy that needed to be addressed.

While some adult children can be impetuous and want to leave relationships too quickly, it can take a long time before it occurs to adult children that they can leave a relationship that is not making them happy. Just like a child, their overriding feeling is that they need to change their own behaviour in order to improve the situation ('If I were better, it would be better'). When their partners behave in a disappointing or dishonouring way, the adult child takes the behaviour personally ('I am not good enough') rather than understanding that it's their partner who is unreliable or not good enough. Because of their fear of not being good enough, adult children often can't understand why their partners want to be with them in the first place, and they do the eggshell walk, trying to do everything just right so that their partners do not realise what a mistake they have made by being with them. They are so busy trying not to be left that they do not consider the possibility that they may want to do the leaving.

Harriet, an adult child extraordinaire, is very intuitive and has physical responses to many situations that she would otherwise be oblivious to. She had such an intense reaction to her husband's mother and his children from a previous marriage that she could not go to their houses, nor could she have them in her own house. She hated them with such passion it was almost amusing. But the constant blind eye she turned to her husband and his lack of interest in or support of her was nothing short of heartbreaking. Eventually, she got tired of supporting him and his children, and being left alone every weekend while he went fishing with his friends, and kicked him out of the house she had bought for them. Within a few days of his departure, she discovered that he had been having an affair for years – which might go some way to explaining his fishing weekends and complete lack of interest in her physically. Devastated for a week or two, she soon noticed that her almost ever-present migraine had disappeared and that, miraculously, the weight she had been battling to shed for many years started to melt away effortlessly. Not because she was unhappy, she explained to me, but because she didn't need the extra layer of protection from her now ex-husband and his toxic family anymore.

What many adult children struggle with is recognising what is reasonable for them to expect from a partner, and Harriet was no exception. She knew something (actually lots of things) did not feel right in her marriage, but because she did not expect to feel happy, she put up with an unhappy marriage for far longer than she should have done.

It can be very confusing to be in a relationship with an adult child. Just as the relationship seems to be going fine and to have reached a level of intimacy, trust and fun that bodes well for the future, the adult child may take fright, remember their fears of being abandoned, being not good enough, or of losing themselves, and withdraw from the relationship. As hard as it is for the adult child to be in a relationship, it is equally challenging for their partners, who may not have had a similar childhood, and who may find the unpredictability of their partner confounding at best, and hurtful and rejecting at worst.

The relationship sabotaging behaviours that some adult children are (unconsciously) compelled to engage in stem from their personal experience of love – or lack thereof – as children.

Roger yearned to be in a relationship with someone who would live with and nurture him, and provide a safe haven for him when he got home from his stressful workplace. He started dating and met a woman who seemed perfect for him. He was really excited about her at first, loving her happiness and interest in him. Almost without him noticing, he started to see more and more of her and began to feel quite attached. Then a childlike terror kicked in and he took fright and started to detach. He started being less available to his girlfriend, stopped calling when he said he would, and grew more and more irritable with her when they were together. Essentially, Roger was hoping that she would break up with him, thereby proving that all women are untrustworthy and heart-breakers. Luckily this particular girlfriend did not give up so easily and was able to stick it out while Roger made sense of his adult child fears and self-sabotaging behaviours, and they made it through that rough patch. Of course there will be other rough patches – there always are – but they were confident that they would be able to navigate their way through those, too, by getting help if necessary.

Everyone has needs and expectations that relationships should meet; the need to be seen, to be heard, to share, to feel love, to be loved in return. Adult children, however, often have needs that are neither straightforward nor constructive. Stemming from those deep-seated fears and unconscious behaviour patterns may also be the need for approval, for attention, even for excitement and danger, as well as a need to be needed.

Each of these needs can have a negative impact on the adult child and their relationships. A need to be needed not only encourages the adult child to deny or to ignore his or her own needs and desires in a relationship, but also takes away the opportunity for their partner to look after themselves. This can feel overwhelming and stifling for a partner, particularly if they are strong and whole. Similarly, the needs for approval and attention can place undue strain on a relationship because the partner of the adult child may feel that they are the partner of the child aspect more than the adult.

Who Are You in Love?

Human interaction is a little like an onion. There are many layers to it, and every time we reveal one layer, there seem to be more layers lurking below. All families unconsciously assign roles to each member of the family and I'm sure you'll recognise a couple of these: the 'good' daughter, the 'rebellious' son, the 'clever' one, the 'sensitive' one …

Children raised in healthy, predictable homes with open and honest communication are able to be flexible and spontaneous and adapt the role they play according to the situation in which they find themselves. Children growing up in chaotic or unhappy families often become stuck in a role that they adopted in order to get through their childhood with some stability and security.

Claudia Black, author of *It Will Never Happen to Me!*, has identified three 'roles' that adult children tend to adopt: '*the responsible one*', '*the adjuster*' and '*the placator*'. Just as adult children tend to adopt a role in their family of origin so, too, do they adopt a role in their intimate relationships.

The Responsible One

This is the 'little adult' of the family. The responsible ones present as being mature beyond their years. They take responsibility for whatever there is to be taken care of, both materially and emotionally. These children become parents to themselves, their siblings and to their parents. They cook and clean, discipline younger children and even try to solve their parents' marital problems. They are almost always anxious and worried, and never feel good enough.

In adulthood, they carry on trying to control their environment and everyone in it. They are uncomfortable with emotions because they see having feelings as being out of control or weak, so they never stop long enough to reflect on their own emotional state. They learn that other people's feelings and happiness are more important than their own. They are others-centredness personified.

These 'little adults' generally grow up to be successful and 'together' but behind this front is a person who is completely out of touch with who they really are. Most of the time they are struggling to be happy, to develop and maintain healthy and fulfilling relationships, and are often insecure and lonely. They frequently suffer from depression, stress and burnout as a result of living for other people and not for themselves.

They find it hard to let go, have fun, and trust that they don't have to do it all by themselves.

Gina is the responsible one in her family and in her relationship. She is the only one in her family who has continued to study after finishing high school. She has a good job and uses her salary to support her parents and her siblings, as well as herself and her own child and partner. She is the family social worker and is constantly being called in to sort out various crises, dramas and arguments among her family and friends. Although she has a wonderful husband who is kind and supportive, Gina continues to bear the brunt of the financial and emotional security in her relationship with him, too.

The Adjuster

This is the child who is able to adjust to whatever situation they find themselves in. They seem not to be emotionally invested in the family and are able to shrug off events by saying 'Nothing makes any difference anyway' and 'I don't care ... it doesn't bother me.' They are the proverbial ducks off whose backs water runs. They spend much of their time trying to avoid being noticed. They are sometimes referred to as the 'lost child' as they are able emotionally to detach to the point where they are completely out of touch with their own feelings and needs.

In adulthood, this pattern has significant implications for the adjuster who lives life without emotional information about feelings and needs. They will find themselves in situations they don't really want to be in, and which can cause them immense unhappiness. They tend to adjust quickly to a bad situation, and because they are used to coping with adversity they 'tough things out' rather than risk changing their situation. They typically will never really stop to ask 'What do I need?' or 'What would be best for me?' They find it hard to allow themselves to change their minds, or to do things for themselves, but easily go along with changes made by others.

David is an adjuster. Growing up, his father was emotionally and physically abusive, and David learned to let the hurt that was inflicted on him simply roll over and off him. After years of trying to avoid pain, David is now almost impervious to his own discomfort in any situation. For some time he has been in a relationship that does not serve or suit him, but he can't seem to summon up the energy required to end it. He has a stressful job in a high-performance organisation that is being severely affected by the recession. Although it is pretty clear that he is under enormous strain at work, he shrugs off all the tension and anxiety that he must be feeling in the face of a very possible retrenchment and says things like 'I don't care if they fire me. It doesn't bother me at all.' David has developed the art of adjusting to whatever life throws at him by pretending to himself and everyone around him that he doesn't care what happens to him.

The Placator

This is the household 'social worker', the child who takes responsibility for the emotional well-being of the whole family. If this is you, you will recognise making it your responsibility to reduce and minimise the expressed and unexpressed fears, sadness, anger and embarrassment of the whole family. As a child you will have been the one to intervene in household arguments, trying desperately to smooth things over. These children are generally warm, caring, empathic young people and are very good at not drawing attention to themselves as children in need.

Placators are far too involved in focusing on other family

members' needs, in an often desperate attempt to try and control what happens in the family. These children feel responsible for the emotional well-being of others but they are inadequately prepared to provide it. They are constantly worried and tense as they wait for the next crisis.

As an adult, the placator embraces others-centredness and spends all available energy in meeting others' needs and ignoring his or her own emotions and needs. They often appear emotionally exhausted, listless and depressed and it's not uncommon for them to resort to pills or substances to cope. They take responsibility for the pain of others, and tend to take care of their partner's need before their own. They are good at giving but struggle with accepting love, care and attention.

Grace is not yet thirty but already she has the air of an old woman, disillusioned by life around her. Her husband of five years is in remission from the cancer he has been battling since shortly after they got married, but she still worries that he is going to die. She phones him every two hours to check that he has eaten, taken his vitamins, is warm enough. If it starts to rain, she phones him to check that he has managed to stay dry. Her whole life revolves around making sure her husband is okay. Her work is suffering and she is exhausted and depressed. She is so used to acting as the placator – a role she developed as the child of parents who argued a lot – that she has forgotten how to placate herself. Interestingly, but unsurprisingly, as soon as Grace stops trying to regulate her husband's every move and thought, he starts to take more responsibility for himself, and is able to start looking after her a bit too.

In addition to these three roles, there are a couple of 'sub-roles' that adult children learn to play in their families:

The 'acting out child' or scapegoat is the child who is the most noticed, the one who – like the canary in the mines – lets people know that there is a problem. Their 'delinquent' behaviour is a reflection of the chaos the child is experiencing at home, and unfortunately often continues into adulthood, primarily in addictive or antisocial behaviours.

Then there is the 'clown' who tries to draw attention away from the difficulties and tensions at home by being funny and cute and providing a distraction for the members of the family and also for the outsiders looking in. They are the ones who are always playing the fool at home and at work, trying to lighten any tense atmosphere or situation that they feel uncomfortable in by being silly and distracting.

For adult children who have assumed one or some of these roles in their families of origin (often unconsciously), it is a natural extension to play the same roles in their relationships. It is often hard for an adult child to recognise that they are playing out these roles, and therefore to be able to shrug off that role and to assume an equal, adult role in relation to their partners.

Role Play

What role do you generally assume in relationships? Are you an adjuster, a placator or a responsible person? Maybe you are a clown or – less likely if you are reading this book – a scapegoat? Or do you have a combination of these roles? How do you think your playing your role impacts on your ability to have your own needs met in your intimate relationships?

Adult Children Out of Love

As we know, the often misplaced sense of loyalty that adult children have can make it just as difficult for them to leave a relationship, as it is for them to be in one. When a relationship does end, it is very hard for adult children to let go of it and move on in a healthy and integrated way. The habit of looking at what might have been rather than what was and to second guess themselves can prove to be disintegrating for adult children who have ended a relationship.

They may torment themselves with thoughts about what they could have done to make it work, and what they might have done to make it fail. And it does feel like *their* failure, rather than a relationship that was not suitable or might have just run its natural course. There may also be a temptation to glorify their ex-partner, and see them as perfect and wonderful, to 'remember' them as the person the adult child wished they could be, rather than who they really were.

Lindi did that for a few months after she ended her relationship with her cheating fiancé. She would beat herself up regularly and rue the day she kicked him out of her house. She went through a period of feeling that she had made a terrible mistake, that she would never find anyone as handsome, clever, kind, charismatic or sexy as the faithless Ben. She was too quick to judge. She shouldn't have thrown him out without letting him explain himself. Inevitably, she allowed herself to start seeing him again. She let him take her out for lunches, then she let him visit her at home, then he started to drop in late at night. And every time she saw him she felt more conflicted. She knew she was right to not trust him but the adult child in her kept making excuses and seeing past his unreliability to the pain that she was sure was causing it all. For some time, she allowed her faith in his potential to override her common sense and her intuition.

As Lindi got stronger and more Adult, she started to recognise that his behaviour, however deep-seated in pain and disappointment it may have been, was just not good enough for her. She managed to put a stop to his game-playing by telling him she did not want to have any contact with him for a while, and she gave herself the time and space to heal her bruised ego and heart. Gradually she stopped taking responsibility for the demise of the relationship and finally allowed herself to see that perhaps the copious amounts of cocaine the much revered Ben had been stuffing up his nose might have had more to do with the end of their relationship than anything she had or had not done.

☆

The ability to make excuses for and not see the truth about others and their behaviours serves only to allow the adult child to confirm their worst fears that they are not good enough, and if they had been better then so would the relationship have been better. In response to this confirmation, the adult child either rushes headlong into another relationship to try and get it right this time (a bit like a compulsive gambler who keeps losing poker hands but can't quit), or retreats into a safe space and does not let anyone in for a very long time.

Janet was sent to boarding school against her will when she was a teenager, resulting in the development of her core Survivor Self belief that she will be sent away if she is not good enough. So scary is this thought that she had not one but two unsuitable and unsatisfactory boyfriends when she came to see me. She was so terrified of being alone and feeling abandoned that she kept herself running between these two men, neither of whom – unsurprisingly, given the circumstances – gave her the attention and permanence she craved. Too frightened to be alone, it took months of introspection and work before Janet was able to provide for herself the emotional security she had been looking for outside of herself. It sounds too good to be true but the fact is that when she did reach the point of being able to love herself the way she wanted to be loved, and managed finally to leave both of her boyfriends, she very quickly met a wonderful man with whom she is now in a healthy and happy relationship.

All Wrongs are One Step Closer to Right

In order to move forward and have healthy and happy relationships, it is helpful to take some time to think about past relationships, and see if you can identify any patterns or themes in the attitudes and behaviours of your previous partners, and in your responses to them. When you get clear about recognising our self-sabotaging behaviours and limiting beliefs, it is possible to put a stop to them and seek out positive, enjoyable and creative experiences.

It's time to take up your journal again and this time I want you to make your own 'Clarity through Contrast' worksheet to help you develop a picture of the kind of relationship you would like to have. On the left-hand side of a page, list all the things, qualities, behaviours, attitudes, etc, about your previous (and current) relationships that have NOT worked for you. Then, in the right-hand column, turn this around and write a quality, behaviour, etc, that you DO want in your relationship. For example:

Contrast	Clarity
Doesn't call when s/he says s/he will	Someone who is reliable and does what s/he says s/he will do
Forgets my birthday	Always remembers important dates and anniversaries
Isn't kind to my children	Makes an effort with my kids
Doesn't like my dogs	Loves animals

Then, turn the points in the clarity column into a narrative description of the relationship you would like to have, like this:

'I want to be in a relationship with someone who is reliable and trustworthy and always does what s/he says s/he will do. I want my partner to remember things that are important to me and honour my birthday and our anniversary. S/he must make an effort with my children and pets and must like animals ...'

This exercise will help you to recognise what does not work for you, in order for you to avoid it in the future, while giving you an idea of what to look for in a relationship and work towards.

Becoming conscious and aware of our patterns of behaviour and thoughts helps us to change them.

Healthy in Love

In the book *Women Who Love Too Much* (a book that I think is equally relevant for adult children of both genders), Robin Norwood draws a link between growing up in a dysfunctional family, and experiencing difficulties with having healthy adult relationships. It is very possible and very common, however, for adult children to overcome their challenges and be healthy in love and in life. Many of my clients are justifiably proud of the healthy relationships that they are in.

In order to achieve this, basic self-love and self-regard are required, even while you may be wanting to continue to grow and develop. Everything starts from there. You should reach a stage where you accept yourself – including aspects of yourself such as your sexuality and sexual orientation. You should be able to validate yourself rather than look to someone else for self-worth.

Adult children often struggle with allowing themselves to be, and to enjoy being, in relationships with people who are healthy and have a healthy self-esteem of their own; in relationships where there is no need to be needed. Healthy adults in relationships have a clear sense of boundaries but also allow themselves to be open and trusting; they can be intimate in all senses of the word. They are in relationships that they choose to be in because they are healthy and generative, and if they choose to leave a relationship that is not longer good for them, they can do so with relative ease and not feel devastated, worthless and alone.

Healthy adults in relationships value continuity and calm over drama and chaos – they do not need to seek out crises to feel alive. It is important to accept those around them, without trying to change them into who they want them to be.

Alison is an adult child whose marriage has been unhappy for years. Sometimes she plays the Child to his Parent, sometimes the Parent to his Child. More often than their children would like, they are both Children, but they are never both Adults. It is deeply frustrating and Alison has been unhappy for a long time. But her husband is an important man and very rich, and she is bound by a sense of duty to keep up the facade of a happy marriage for her children, her social circle and her financial well-being.

Like many adult children who finally allow themselves to realise how unhappy they are in their relationship, Alison wanted to leave her marriage as quickly as possible, but as we worked together she came to realise that she was just as much a part of the problem as her husband. Her conditioning has made her distrustful of her own ideas and strength, and her anger with herself and her husband at allowing their marriage to reach a point where she feels almost totally disempowered was making her incredibly passive-aggressive and sabotaging. She and her husband were locked in a dance of disappointment, anger and undermining of each other. It was truly horrible to hear about, and I can't even imagine how unpleasant it must have been to be a part of.

The easy approach would have been to leave and to start again, but Alison took the brave route, and went through a coaching programme that allowed her to recognise her own limiting beliefs and behaviours, and empowered her to take on an Adult role. Instead of going along with her husband when he suggested something she did not want to do, she suggested something else calmly, rationally, and from her Adult state. Instead of getting frustrated with him for not knowing what she wanted to do on the weekends, she started to tell him by making suggestions about how they could spend the time together.

Slowly but surely over the weeks Alison's husband started to respond to her from his own Adult state, and Alison began to remember what she loved about him, and about their relationship. It was not easy, and it will not be easy for some time, because they have to relearn how to be with each other; they have to accept each other and acknowledge each other for who they really are rather than who they would like each other to be. But it is possible, and for Alison each day it gets a little easier.

Making the shift from adult child in relationships to Adult in relationships is a challenge, but it can be done. Understanding and becoming conscious of the limiting beliefs and fears that underpin self-sabotaging patterns of behaviour allow us to choose another path. With constant consciousness, and vigilance, adult children can use their self-awareness and self-knowledge to help them make decisions about how to move forward in relationships, even (or especially) if moving forward means leaving behind relationships that are not healthy.

To change your life, you must change your story.

Please Please Yourself

Adult children often look to other people, and this includes their intimate partner, to make them feel happy and whole, rather than creating those feelings in themselves. What can you do to make yourself feel happier and more fulfilled?

Take your journal and identify at least 20 small things that you can do for yourself that make you feel good. Some examples might be to have a bubble bath, stay in with a book and a bar of chocolate, go for a walk with the dog, take yourself off for a massage ... And then do ONE A DAY from now on. In loving yourself you are setting an example for how you want to be loved by others.

6

Adult Children at Work

I have had many clients who fit onto the adult child continuum, and many of them feel unhappy at work; unfulfilled, misunderstood, bored, overwhelmed, mistrustful, taken for granted and so on. Interestingly, a number of them have felt this way in every job they have ever had, which suggests that *they* are the common denominator, rather than the work situations in which they find themselves.

It is important to mention that some adult children struggle to find work and a work environment that 'fits' them, and so they may find it difficult to commit to one course of action in the work context. The pressure to succeed or to excel that adult children place on themselves may prove to be too much, and can result in immobilising them. They may have a problem deciding what work to do, where to do it, or who to do it with, and this indecision can result in an ever-changing work-landscape for some adult children. For the purposes of this chapter, however, we are going to be examining adult children who are in a relatively stable work situation, but the lessons are equally applicable to these 'rolling stone' adult children workers too.

I am sure by now you will have clearly recognised how your experience as a child is reflected in your adult relationships, and how this also applies in other areas of your life. Because work is such a big part of our lives and is another arena in which we form our identity, it is also an area in which many adult children feel challenged. The characteristics, limiting beliefs and behaviours that inform how adult children behave are as evident in the workplace as anywhere else.

Sigmund Freud famously said that 'Love and work are the cornerstone of our humanness'. They are where we invest most of our time and energy, and where we give expression to ourselves. For many adult children, work is an environment that incubates and exacerbates their difficulties with interacting in the world. Because work is such an important and – for those of us who are fortunate – meaningful expression of who we are, many of our insecurities and anxieties play themselves out in the workplace. Limiting beliefs such as 'I am not good enough', 'If I were better, it would be better' and 'I can't ask for help' have a field day in the work context.

The hierarchical nature of organisations, no matter how hard some companies try to build 'flat' structures, closely resembles the family system: managers are the parents, peers are the siblings, and subordinates the children. Almost inevitably for adult children, unconscious thought and behaviour patterns, developed in childhood, are reflected back at them in the office.

Alex is a hesitant young woman, with big brown eyes and an unassuming air. She had a violent father and a passive mother.

'When my manager calls me into his office,' she tells me, 'I get so scared. I think he is going to shout at me and humiliate me. I am even scared that he is going to hurt me. But sometimes it feels even worse when he is not cross with me and wants to compliment me.'

Whenever anyone in the family did something to displease Dad, or even just when he was in a bad mood or had had too much to drink, Alex's father would beat the object of his frustration with his fists and a belt. Not just violent, he was also emotionally manipulative. Alex remembers how her father used to make an example of whichever of the five children did best at school, showering him or her with praise and telling the sisters and brothers that they needed to be more like their sibling. As a result Alex feels very uncomfortable when she is singled out for praise by her manager.

Remembering the destructive rivalry that her father used to set up and encourage between her and her sisters and brothers, she is much happier when everyone is treated exactly the same and it feels as though everyone is appreciated equally. She tries not to draw attention to herself and has remained in the same role for much longer than she should have. The fear of being made an example of has made her resist applying for any promotions; she'd rather be left to play nicely with the other children.

Depending on how they related to their parents, the adult child at work may feel the need to look after their manager, or be needed by them, or possibly even be constantly asserting their own independence and autonomy. If they played a nurturing role towards their brothers and sisters, they may find themselves being the office social worker or agony aunt, listening to all their colleagues' problems, dispensing advice, even on occasion doing others' work for them.

Adult children have difficulty standing up for themselves and this is particularly evident at work. Fearing rejection, maybe in the form of being fired or not getting an increase, adult children often find themselves putting their hands up for all kinds of tasks and responsibilities, even if they do not have enough time or don't feel equipped to do the job. And it seldom occurs to them to ask for help if they are not sure how to do something, or even if they need practical assistance and support. Those people who take their work home with them and always seem to be behind with deadlines may not necessarily be the work addict their family and friends think they are; they are in all likelihood adult children too scared or anxious to stop and ask for help.

Or maybe they are like Lindi, doing her own work and also completing many of the tasks her colleague was too lazy or uncommitted to do. Lindi was so scared that if the work was not done, it would reflect badly on her and she would get into trouble for her colleague's tardiness, that she used to complete her colleague's work during office hours and spend long evenings and most of the weekends doing her own work which she never seemed to have enough time to do properly while at the office.

Performance appraisals, no one's favourite part of work, can be paralysingly frightening for adult children. They do not feel like it's their work that is being appraised, but rather they themselves. Because they struggle to see where they end and where everything and everyone else begins, they tend to take feedback very personally and to be easily devastated by criticism, however gentle and constructive. An adult child can receive mostly excellent ratings on their job performance feedback, but just throw in one 'could do better' and they will be devastated. They will move right past the 'excellents' and focus on their disappointment at being recognised as 'not good enough'. Adult children do not see this as one aspect of their *work* that could be improved on. For them it as a clear message that it is they themselves who are lacking.

Cindy came for coaching to help her prepare for her annual performance appraisal meeting. She was feeling very anxious about it. It soon became clear that she loved almost every aspect of her job and that she was very good at meeting most of her responsibilities. She had no worries about her appraisal when it came to ninety per cent of what she did, but she was terrified about her evaluation in one performance area: stats. She hates doing the monthly statistical analyses that her job requires.

Maybe she is not very good at them because she hates them so much, or maybe she hates them so much because she is not very good at them. Whichever came first is not as relevant as the fact that Cindy battles on with trying to make sense of those figures, alone, scared and very unhappy, month after month. Twelve times a year, for a few days leading up to the process, the two days required to do the analyses, and the day it takes to write the report, Cindy is a wreck. She can't enjoy any other part of her life – personal or professional – because the anxiety about the stats is constantly lurking in the back of her mind. Her worry is that she will get something wrong – and she often does, which serves only to make her more panic-stricken the following month.

Fighting my desire to suggest that she find a job that doesn't involve numbers of any kind (we call that 'projection' in my line of work), I put on my best problem solving voice and ask Cindy how she thinks she could improve the experiences – both the performance appraisal discussion around her stats reports, and the actual writing of the reports. She has no idea.

And she is not being difficult; she really *has* no idea. Like so many adult children, she is so used to making the best of a bad situation and getting on with things that it does not occur to her that there may be possible alternatives to her monthly torment and anguish.

'Is there anyone you could ask for help?' I suggest rather tentatively, fairly sure that she will say no without even really thinking about it.

Cindy does not disappoint. 'No,' she says flatly. 'It is my job and my responsibility and I have to do it.'

Adult children, so quick to look after and help others, are often so very bad at looking after and helping themselves. Cindy has painted herself into a proverbial corner here; she has agreed to do something she hates and is not good at, and she refuses to ask for help. With every indication that she could do better, she feels less worthy and worse about herself, and less able to ask for help.

It takes some time and a good few sessions, but eventually Cindy does come to see what she is doing to herself and finally allows herself to ask for help. After this breakthrough she told me at the next session that she had taken the initiative and raised her difficulty with stats in the performance appraisal meeting, and that she and her supervisor had identified a colleague who was happy to work with Cindy every month until she was confident enough to make sense of the stats and compile the reports on her own.

Asking for help seems so simple from the outside, but for adult children who feel as though they are stuck in a situation over which they have no control and little or no choice, it can feel impossible to admit they need help.

Ask for Help

Think about at least one thing that you can ask for help with – start small with asking for directions or maybe advice. Now identify someone who you think may be able to help you. You know what you need to do next . . .

Because they are so eager to please, and to be seen and loved, adult children are mostly dream employees. They may have some difficulty with authority and not like to be told what to do, but those adult children who hold down jobs and work hard are difficult to beat as model workers. Because they cannot easily say no, and often feel an almost overwhelming need to be needed, adult children are sometimes exploited and taken advantage of by supervisors and co-workers.

The crisis-oriented living which is so familiar to many adult children may also make them very good at working under pressure, resulting in them being assigned to difficult and demanding projects. Because of the need to be in control and to be reliable and responsible, they may also find themselves agreeing to tackle projects and tasks they would rather not take on, but that they do not trust others to do either. Many adult children will want to do all or nothing. Because of their lack of trust in other people doing what they say they will, adult children find it hard to delegate, preferring to do much of the work themselves. Is it any wonder that so many adult children develop burnout?

The unconscious belief 'If I were better, it would be better' is the reason why so many adult children are vulnerable to becoming scapegoats at work. They will all too quickly assume responsibility and blame when things go wrong or not according to plan (which can often happen when they're overburdened with too many responsibilities).

As we now know, adult children take themselves very seriously and struggle to have fun and this can manifest in the workplace, with the adult child finding it difficult to socialise with colleagues and engage in workplace banter. This may serve to alienate them from their colleagues, and make them even more vulnerable to being a scapegoat when things go pear shaped.

Adult children also tend to feel responsible when disappointed, which makes it virtually impossible for them to not feel that it is their fault if something does not go according to plan at work. Adult children who have been retrenched during uncertain economic times, for example, will almost certainly feel that it is because they are not good enough, rather than being able to recoginse that the world economic downturn is at fault.

Charles runs a medium sized business which has been hard hit by the uncertain economic climate. He has tried his best to keep all his staff members employed, but has not been able to keep jobs for three people. Having to retrench them was devastating for Charles. Despite knowing all that he had done to support them and try to help them find new positions, he felt that he was not good enough and a failure. It was only when each of the three people told him that they had found other jobs that Charles was able to feel better and put down his guilt about having to let them go.

The difficulty that many adult children have with completing long-term projects may be very pronounced in the workplace. Big tasks may seem overwhelming and adult children can easily feel discouraged by the minor setbacks and challenges that are inevitable with any project. Combined with the need to be perfect and the horror of unanticipated changes to the plan, typical project teething problems may result in the adult child either wanting to hand over their responsibilities to someone else or stop the project altogether, or possibly even leave the company. But then their loyalty issues kick in, and despite fantasising about running away, they mostly stay and try to get things right, always feeling responsible when things go awry. What's that refrain you hear running through your head? Oh yes – 'If I were better, it would be better'.

Roger, whom we met earlier on, existed in a constant state of anxiety about all the things he could not anticipate, control, or eliminate at work. Even when he wasn't at work he was worrying about work. Change is one of the only constants in the sector he works in, and things go wrong all the time; it is part of the learning curve that electronic industries accept as being part and parcel of the work that they do. But for Roger, each unexpected development, every glitch in the system made him feel inadequate and not good enough. It was only after he learned to separate himself from his work, and to see that a setback at work was not a reflection on him personally, that he was able to relax and start to enjoy the work that he was so good at.

Although they are very good at feeling guilty and responsible when things do not go well, adult children are generally very bad at accepting and believing compliments and positive feedback from supervisors and co-workers, and they often downplay their achievements. This, combined with the need for approval and affirmation, can result in a constant dance of approval seeking and rebutting between adult children and their colleagues.

The truth is that adult children never feel quite good enough wherever they are. In the workplace this may manifest as something I call the 'moving target' syndrome. Nod your head if this sounds like you: you're sure you will feel competent and okay in your work world if you could just complete the next project well, or land that next big job, or get that next promotion. You look for evidence of how much you still 'need' to get right, rather than acknowledging what you are already doing well.

Not feeling good enough has obvious implications for adult children when asking for a salary raise or applying for promotion.

☆

Once again, limiting beliefs – variations on the general ones we have already looked at, and some that are specific to the world of work – that unconsciously drive many adult children's thoughts and actions are very evident at work.

Adult children put themselves under enormous pressure to get along well with everyone at work; bosses and colleagues alike. If there is a slightly tricky relationship, they are quick to feel that they are the cause because of the idea that 'I am responsible when someone disappoints me'. If there is a difficult relationship with a boss or co-worker, adult children often believe that it is because they are doing something wrong or not well enough.

Sophie has recently been appointed to a team that was without a formal leader for a few months while her appointment was being finalised. When she took up her position as team leader, Ned, who had been a self-appointed leader in the meantime, was not impressed. He tried everything to undermine Sophie, disagreeing with her in meetings, cancelling meetings at the last minute, trying to stir discontent among the rest of the team. Sophie was devastated. Being the kind, empathic and sensitive adult child she is, she had gone out of her way to try and make everyone on the team feel equally important and valued, and Ned's passive aggression was eroding all her confidence in herself and her ability to do her job. She was sure there was something she was doing wrong and that was why he was behaving so badly. It was only when the team was involved in a larger organisational meeting in which Ned was taken to task by the meeting leader for being disruptive, that Sophie realised that his divisive behaviour was a reflection on him rather than on her.

Adult children are conditioned from early on to prove their worth and to make other people happy, often at their own expense. It often does not occur to them to think how they may be able to make work work for them, rather than for their boss, colleagues or family.

All Michael ever wanted to be was a minister in his church. After school he went away to a seminary to study to become a preacher. But two years into his three-year degree, he got a call from his family. They had seen an advert for a job they felt would be perfect for him and they wanted him to apply for it. They very badly needed the money his salary would provide. Against every instinct that he had, Michael agreed to send in his application and he got the job, as his family had hoped and he had feared.

He left the seminary, and moved again to take up the post. 'It is not that I hate what I do at all,' he explained to me, 'it is just that it isn't what I really want to do and I feel as though I have failed myself.'

He was the only member of his extended family who was employed, and he did not feel that he could leave his work just then. He did reach the realisation, though, that he didn't have to choose one or the other option, and that it was perfectly feasible to do both. Last time I saw him he was still at his day job, was finishing his Bible Studies part-time and was preaching every weekend as a lay preacher at his local church.

Just like in every other area of their lives, adult children live in constant (often unconscious) fear of being 'outed' as not good or worthy enough in their jobs. And if they are recognised as imperfect then they may well be rejected, replaced or humiliated.

Nandi was constantly worried about not doing a good enough job. When we talked about what fuelled this fear, she realised that, without being aware of it, she was scared that if she got something wrong she would be hurt. Her childhood experience of being beaten by her father every time she made a mistake had come with her to work, and was making it very hard for her to do her job properly.

Lance, who has created such a good name for himself in the sector he works in, finds it almost impossible to say no when he is asked if he is available to do a particular job. Even if he hates the work that he is being asked to do, can't bear the people he will have to work with, and already has too much other work to complete, he still says yes because he is so anxious about not being asked again, and being replaced, if he says no.

Cindy tried to avoid what felt to her to be certain humiliation if she admitted she needed help with her stats reports for many long tortuous months. It was in her job description so she must be able to do it. Interestingly, Cindy was very quick to share the things she was good at. When she was praised for a good report she deflected the praise on to her colleagues, giving far more importance and credit to their input than was deserved.

Adult children are quick to accept blame when something goes wrong, but slow to take credit when something goes right. Although adult children crave being noticed and appreciated, they struggle with accepting praise and recognition. 'It was nothing' is a very common response. 'Anyone could have done it.'

These are just some of the many limiting beliefs that underlie some of the fear-based behaviours of adult children employees. They are all variations of the same themes that have been discussed up to now, but are profoundly influential in the adult child's attitude to work, and their feelings about themselves at work.

Boundaries and Business

Adult children often battle with clear boundaries, and the workplace is no exception. Adult children, who are so used to trying to change themselves to improve the environment, often struggle to differentiate between the workplace being chaotic, and themselves not being good enough. Rather than seeing the faults in the environment, adult children almost always believe that the fault is with them.

An over-involvement in other people's problems may result in professional boundaries being compromised. Being overly responsible and needing to be needed leaves the adult child open to exploitation by co-workers and supervisors, and can even make them vulnerable to sexual harassment, or occasionally inappropriate sexual relationships, in the workplace.

Adult children who are otherscentered at home often are at work, too. They can find themselves being the informal 'social worker' at work, and taking on special care-taking relationships with troubled colleagues. The need to be needed can manifest in an interest in and support of colleagues who have difficulties with their personal lives or with professional problems.

Adult children may enable their co-workers by picking up the slack when they are not doing their part. Lindi was behaving in a very codependent way when she was covering for her under-performing colleague, even though she hated the colleague and resented the extra work.

Perhaps the most difficult manifestation of the problem with boundaries at work is the adult child's struggle to recognise where they end and where someone else begins. This can result in blurred boundaries and over-involvement in other people's issues and problems – getting involved in other people's business.

Byron Katie is a woman who has a world view that is incredibly sophisticated in its simplicity. The author of a number of books, including *Loving What Is*, and the creator of a powerful method of 'enquiry' called 'The Work' that questions thoughts and beliefs, her ideas and processes have brought relief from painful thoughts to countless people.

Katie says that she can find only three types of 'business' in the universe: mine, yours and God's. She explains that a great deal of the stress we experience comes from mentally living out of our own business. When we imagine what other people should think, do or feel, we are in their business. And when we worry about poverty, war, floods and death, we are in God's business.

'If I am mentally in your business or in God's business, the effect is separation … Being mentally in your business keeps me from being present in my own. I am separate from myself, wondering why my life doesn't work. To think that I know what's best for anyone else is to be out of my business.'

Because of how they grew up, adult children often struggle to stay in their own business and this can be a particular challenge in the workplace. Not trusting that colleagues can or will do their jobs properly, and feeling guilty about 'imposing' on them by asking them to complete difficult or unpleasant tasks, may make the adult child shoulder much more responsibility than they need to. In conversation with many of my adult child clients who are experiencing burnout, it emerges that much of their exhaustion and overwhelm is a result of undertaking not just their own roles at work, but also many of the responsibilities of their colleagues and subordinates.

For people like Lindi, getting into other people's business can become a vicious cycle. The less Lindi trusted the people around her to do their work, the more she did the work that wasn't hers to do, and the less able the people whose responsibility it was to do the work became. And the less time Lindi had to do her own work and get the recognition and praise she both deserved and craved.

Mind Your Own Business

When you start feeling anxious or stressed about a colleague or situation at work, try to take a step back and ask yourself, 'Whose business am I in?' If it doesn't belong to you, don't get involved.

Try to think of times and situations when you have acted on the urge to get involved in other people's (or even God's) business and have jumped in boots and all. Write down all the times you can remember doing this, and see if you can discern any recurring patterns. Also, see if it has or hasn't served you to get involved in other people's business.

Adult children who are in management roles may assume a Critical Parent stance, and demand compliance because they think that poor performance is a direct reflection on them.

Alternately, adult children supervisors can become Nurturing Parents and 'cover up' and make excuses for subordinates for whom they feel sorry. This is often complicated by the fact they want to be liked by everyone, and often get over-involved in their subordinates' lives by trying to help them. Assuming a Parent state at work means that adult children spend a lot of time out of their own business.

Adult children in senior positions at work can also become overly identified with the organisation, taking on the problems and difficulties that their company may be undergoing and experiencing them as their own personal challenges.

Communication at Work

The workplace can feel like a 'home away from home' for a lot of people. For adult children, this is not necessarily a good thing! Unconsciously, they tend to set up their relationships at work the same way they experienced relationships when they were growing up. Co-workers become siblings and managers become parents, and adult children relate to them, and expect to be related to by them, the way they know from childhood. The roles adult children take on in their families of origin, and in their intimate relationships, are played out again in the office. An adult child who takes on the role of the responsible one at home, is generally the responsible one at work.

Ego state transactions are particularly evident in the workplace. At work, all members of staff are, biologically anyway, adults. However, because of the hierarchical nature of most offices, an examination of the communication styles and sub-texts between colleagues will show that there is a lot of communication coming from the Parent and Child states. For adult children, who are so quick to slip into and out of these two states, this is a particular challenge.

Alex, whom we met earlier, was in Child state most of the time when she was at work. Always waiting to get into trouble or to be humiliated or hurt, she was walking on eggshells almost all the time and looking for ways to defend herself should the need arise. Unfortunately for Alex, the more she felt like a Frightened Child, the more her manager responded as a Critical Parent, making Alex more scared and her manager more irritated. Not only was it very unrelaxing, it also meant that Alex was not able to do the best work she was capable of, thereby keeping her in a junior – and more Childlike – position in the company.

'Don't Tell Me What to Do!'

Adult children have a hard time trusting people in authority. This is not surprising, given how untrustworthy many of the authority figures were in their childhood. Unfortunately, even if authorities in later years show that they *are* worthy of confidence and faith, the adult child finds it hard to let go of the childlike mistrust that is so ingrained. People who have issues with authority figures have a habit of picking fights with people who are in positions of power over them (teachers, bosses, anyone who is in a position to tell them what to do).

Part of the problem between Ned and Sophie was that Ned is also an adult child, and was acting out his mistrust and rejection of authority figures at the same time that Sophie was acting out her need to be loved by all her staff members.

Authority issues can result in very uncomfortable relationships between adult child employees and their managers or supervisors because any feedback – constructive or otherwise – may be perceived as a personal attack and detection of the adult child's imperfection. There is nothing as nerve-wracking for an adult child as the threat of being discovered to be imperfect or not good enough, so we may respond defensively or even aggressively in certain situations. Some adult children may find it very difficult to get along with their bosses or supervisors for this reason.

Making Work Work for You

Adult children believe that if they could just find that perfect job, then they would not experience any difficulties at work. They fantasise about what it would be like to go to another job that did not have the same challenges that their current job has. The truth is that they generally need to work out new ways of being at work rather than seeking out new workplaces.

There are many practical things that adult children can do to help improve their experience of the workplace. First off you need to become and remain aware of your patterns of behaviour and how we self-sabotage so that we are able to pre-empt and avert disaster in the workplace. Proper planning, research, asking for help, and setting small, achievable goals, can all help with starting and finishing projects on time rather than procrastinating and/or non-delivery.

Recognise that it is not possible for anyone to do *everything*. An ability to prioritise tasks in terms of both urgency a*nd* importance, will allow you to spend less time on unimportant things, and more time on the important business.

You also need to be able to see the difference between *doing* something and *being* that thing. This will allow you to accept criticism and feedback when it comes to your work without feeling that this is a direct attack. This is a particularly difficult skill, and one which you really do need in order to, as far as possible, distance yourself from the situation and view it from the Adult perspective.

Adult children – not having a good idea of what 'normal' is – guess a lot of the time. They guess at what is expected of them, they guess at what they can expect from others. To be effective and to feel effective in the workplace, adult children need to give themselves permission to ask what is expected of them.

Adult children can easily become overwhelmed and feel stressed and out of control. If you are ticking each of those boxes, it is important to introduce regular – even daily, if you can – stress reduction programmes such as exercise, relaxation techniques and/or someone to speak to in order to unburden yourself. Adult children often struggle with balance, and it is very important that you consciously strive to maintain work-life balance, with not too much focus on one area at the expense of another.

Adult children who believe (and need) themselves to be indispensable are prone to burn-out. Not just once, but repeatedly. Adult children struggle to recognise what is important and therefore find it hard to prioritise tasks, so they treat everything as urgent and important. 'Not knowing what normal is' contributes to the need to over-commit and to over-perform. This is exacerbated if co-workers and managers do notice and appreciate them. The adult child is so grateful to be seen that they will do anything to keep on getting that affirmation, and they often don't know how to say no. They give more than they get, and certainly give more than they have to give, so they get depleted quickly and often.

As an adult child myself I know how debilitating burnout can be, especially when you refuse to allow yourself to recognise it for what it is. Burnout starts off slowly and, if we don't pay attention to the early warning signs, picks up speed very rapidly. If we don't act to address the early symptoms when they first show themselves, burnout can progress into very serious illnesses with long-lasting effects. What starts off as tiring easily, taking longer to recover from mental and physical exertion, needing frequent fixes of sugar, carbohydrates and coffee to jump-start our energy, progresses to sleep disturbances, changes to mood, social withdrawal and increased conflict. If we don't intervene, our burnout becomes entrenched, and can manifest as depression, heart disease, diabetes and worse. You can read more about burnout, why we get it and how to recover from it in my book, *Recover from Burnout: Life lessons to regain your passion and purpose.*

One of the very challenging aspects of burnout is the fact that, the less productive and effective we become, the more we push ourselves to try to regain that effectiveness and productivity. The worse we feel, the harder we are on ourselves.

To protect ourselves from the very real possibility of burnout and to maintain some balance and enjoyment in our lives, we need to learn how to be power*ful* – and how to keep that power – in the workplace. We need to be able to think proactively about what we want to do and where we want to be going, rather than reacting to what comes our way. We need to learn how to take responsibility only for what is ours, rather than for what is everyone else's. We need to be able to **stay in our own business**, and we have to realise that we do have the choice to improve areas of our work that are not making us happy.

The Wheel of Work

This is an adaptation of the popular coaching tool the 'wheel of life' which you may have come across before. In your journal, draw a large circle and divide that circle into eight wedges. Give the wedges the following labels: physical environment, infrastructure, relationship with colleagues, organisational culture, leadership, career advancement prospects, salary and benefits, content of work.

The eight sections of this wheel represent the eight main areas of your work life (if you can think of any that you would prefer to have, then please replace what is here, or add the new ones). Seeing the centre of the wheel as 0 and the outer rim as 10, rank your current level of satisfaction in each area of work by marking the appropriate place on the 'spoke' of the wheel. Now, join the dots and see where you are out of balance.

How smooth is your ride at work? What are the areas that have the lowest ranking? Can you see any glaring areas that need improvement? What actions can you take to improve the ride? Do the highest ranking areas make up for the lowest ranking ones? Are you able to improve your ratings, and make the wheel rounder, by changing anything in your environment?

Now choose any low-ranking area and identify at least three small steps you can take to improve your satisfaction levels in that area.

Once we have identified the areas of least satisfaction in our work, we are able to take steps to feel more satisfied.

Moving On

Despite the fact that adult children often consider leaving their jobs, they opt to stay put a lot of the time. They remain in bad jobs or toxic work environments either because they will persist in hoping for the best despite all evidence to the contrary, or because they think they need to change themselves because they are the problem ('If I were better, it would be better'). It is dificult for adult children to see that, rather than changing themselves, they can change the environment in which they find themselves. They often struggle to recognise or accept that they are no longer children who do not have a choice or the resources to leave a place that is not healthy for them. They may fantasise about leaving, and even voice their desires out loud, but the adult child can be too scared to leave, preferring to stay in an environment that is familiar in its lack of support and appreciation of them because this is what they have known from childhood to be true.

In cases where it *is* appropriate to change the job and the environment, rather than the behaviour, adult children should not be impulsive (as they are prone to being) but should rather be mindful and considered in finding a job that would make them happier.

Instead of taking the first job that is offered (again that fear of saying no), it is important to get clarity on what would really make you happy. What interests you? What are you good at? What skills, training and experience do you have? What kind of job would you like to have? What would make the best use of your skills and experience, and help you to grow and develop? What kind of work would you like to be doing? Who would you like to be working with? What enviroment would you most like to work in? It is just as important to know what you are running towards, as it is to know what you are running away from.

More Wrongs to Make a Right

Using the same tool that you used earlier to get clarity on the kind of relationship you want, now it's time to get clear on your ideal job and work environment. Use the Wheel of Work you created earlier to help you get started.

Contrast	Clarity
Long boring meetings No windows	Short meetings Fresh air and natural light

It may be that your current job is mostly fine, but just needs tweaking to make it 'perfect', or it may be that you want to make a more radical change at some point. Either way, getting clear on what you want, will help you to get it.

It is very helpful to get a clearer idea of the kind of work and environment you would ideally like to work in, but many of us restrict our imaginings to what we already know. And because adult children are so good at making do with what is, they often do not allow themselves to visualise what could be, and follow a dream rather than a safe path. But sometimes if we allow ourselves to indulge our imaginations and take some risks, surprising and deeply satisfying work can result. I would not be writing this book if I had not allowed myself to imagine the possibility of becoming a life coach – a career that could hardly be more different from the research, training and policy development work in crime prevention that I used to do.

Imagine That!

Often we find ourselves doing the work we do because it is what we know and it's what we are good at it, but here's a radical thought: We can find work that is fun and meaningful. Take a few minutes to let your mind play and try and imagine ten different endings to the following statement: *I could imagine being* ...
(For example: I could imagine being ... an artist, or an architect, or a teacher, or a florist.)

Which of the answers felt the most exciting and inspiring? Spend some time thinking about how you could start to make them happen. Remember to try to talk yourself *into* a new job or career path, rather than *out* of one.

7

Moving Forward

This last section is designed to help you move into the next phase, a phase of understanding, forgiveness and gratitude for all that you have experienced and how it has shaped who you have become.

Don't Forget, but do Forgive

Forgiving others can be hard so it is helpful to make a small but important mind shift and think of forgiveness in a different way. Think of forgiveness as something you are giving to yourself. And that *is* what forgiveness is: a gift to yourself. Forgiveness allows us to free ourselves from anger and resentment. It does not mean that we will forget where we've come from, or even that we *should* forget, or that we should ignore what has happened to us, but by forgiving we allow ourselves to let go of the anger that many adult children feel as a consequence of what has happened to us.

Not only is learning how to forgive very freeing, the action of forgiveness has very real physical and emotional health benefits.

Some of the physical gains that have been shown to be associated with forgiveness include reduced blood pressure and pulse rate, reduced risk of stroke or heart attack, a decrease in back and neck pain, and also in headaches. It has also been shown that the immune system is strengthened, and the need for medication is reduced or even removed altogether. People who allow themselves to forgive also report feeling happier and healthier all round and experience improved mental clarity as well as a generally more optimistic outlook on life.

Edward M Hallowell, a psychiatrist on the faculty of Harvard Medical School, wrote the book *Dare To Forgive: The Power of Letting Go and Moving On*, in which he says that it takes guts, wisdom, patience and imagination to reach a point of forgiveness. A useful question that he has identified for people to ask themselves is: **What do you want your suffering to turn into?** Would you rather suffer through pain and disappointment, or learn from it? Would you rather repeat the mistakes and the hurt that give rise to pain, or break the cycle? Would you rather stay static in your life, or grow and expand into the person you deserve to be?

So, how do you forgive?

Hallowell says there are four stages in the forgiveness process:

- ★ pain
- ★ remembering and reflecting
- ★ working to a peaceful place
- ★ moving forward.

When we are processing our pain, we can allow ourselves to feel wronged and to consider how we would like to respond to the physical or emotional injury inflicted on us. Then we need to use our intelligence, experience and values to reflect on what we would most like the pain to turn into. Working our way past the anger and resentment we have felt towards others and towards the situation allows us to work towards finding a peaceful place, and this in turn allows us to take stock and move forward.

Forgiveness is a process that moves us from pain to growth.

It sounds easy when it is presented like this, but for adult children it is often extremely difficult. Because many adult children have spent the better part of their lives making excuses for people, and pretending that things are fine even when they aren't, it is often a challenge for them to even allow themselves to recognise that a degree of forgiveness may be required.

During Amy's first session with me she told me that her childhood had been fine, not totally idyllic but without dysfunction or chaos of any kind. Yet she exhibited all the signs of being an adult child on the far end of the continuum. She was insecure, anxious, overly responsible, would not let anybody do anything for her, and had almost constant stomach problems and frequent headaches. Something was not adding up but I decided to let it go for a while and we focused on working on her limiting beliefs without relating them to the possibility of her having had an unhappy childhood.

At her third session she told me that she had remembered that her father used to drink too much occasionally when she was a child. By her fifth session she had remembered that when she was six her father had left home for two years after his drinking had got out of control and Amy's mother had given him an ultimatum. In her sixth session, she told me (and herself) how scary it had been for her to spend weekends at her father's house when he was drinking and out of control and how there had been no other adult to provide a safe space for her.

Once she had remembered and felt the pain of these experiences Amy was able to get in touch with her anger and sadness, which were both considerable, and then move to understanding what had been going on with her father in order to forgive him and repair her relationship with him – a relationship that she had struggled with for many years without really knowing why.

☆

If you are able to recognise the pain and struggles endured by the grown-ups in your childhood, and realise that everyone does the best they can, it may be easier for you to forgive them. Hallowell says that to get to forgiveness we need to look for the best in others and in ourselves.

So, allow yourself to remember and to identify events or periods that you may need to make sense of in order to move towards forgiveness and beyond. What can you learn from the experiences, and how can you make sure that you don't repeat those mistakes by unwittingly perpetuating that cycle, either as a recipient or a deliverer? What actions can you take to move forward?

South Africa's Truth and Reconciliation Commission, which was held in the mid-to-late 1990s, demonstrated both the power and the value of telling the truth, becoming free from hate and resentment, and forgiving perpetrators of past wrongdoings. While I am not advocating that you have your own mini-TRC in your family, I do encourage you to give yourself the gift of forgiveness.

Forgiving is brave, it is healthy and it is about honouring yourself. Often it is not only their parents or other care-givers adult children need to forgive, but also themselves. Understanding the unconscious beliefs and common behaviours of adult children, and seeing that they are shared by many people who had difficult childhoods will hopefully allow you to stop judging yourself and to stop feeling that it was your fault or that you were not good enough.

The Serenity Prayer has guided many people dealing with recovery from addictions, and destructive behaviour and the impact these behaviours have had on their lives. It is beautiful, simple and wise beyond measure.

God grant me the serenity to accept the things I cannot change;
the courage to change the things I can;
and the wisdom to know the difference.

The things that you *can* change are the way you see yourself, and the way you respond to situations. Understanding the phenomenon of adult children will, I hope, allow you to pardon yourself for not being perfect, and accept that you were powerless to change the situation of your childhood. You can, however, change your current life situation and how you respond to it now.

Making Lemonade

There is an old saying that goes 'when life gives you lemons, make lemonade'. Despite it being simplistic and a little overly optimistic, there are many times when it holds true. Although it can be hard to recognise it at the time, most-if not all-of the unhappy and challenging experiences we have had, will result in something positive sometime in the future.

One of my favourite coaching tools developed by the wonderful Martha Beck is described in her book *Steering by Starlight*. It is called 'Telling Your Life Story Backward'. This tool takes the reader through a process of linking the things for which they are most grateful in their present lives back to a past experience or event that, at the time, seemed devastating and cruelly unnecessary. It is a truly eye-opening exercise because it allows us to see that from every 'negative' experience, many positive things can result.

Our childhoods allow us to develop all sorts of abilities, skills, and talents. It is important for us to recognise and celebrate the many excellent qualities adult children bring to the world.

Let's look at a few of them.

Adult children are extremely loyal and are thus excellent friends, partners and workers. We are reliable, considerate and supportive of the people around us. The ability to 'make allowances and excuses' for people also means that adult children are not judgmental. We make enormous efforts to understand people and the challenges they experience in life. We are quick to see the best in others, and to stand up for people less fortunate than ourselves. We are not easily scared off and are accepting of our friends' and loved ones' weaknesses and challenges.

Adult children are mostly very responsible and, fuelled by our need to get things right and be perfect, we are extremely good employees and colleagues. We work hard, are driven to do well, and our familiarity with chaos and drama can make us very good in a crisis. Although we hate change – especially change over which we have no control – we are responsive to it as well as to unexpected hitches.

I used to work with a wonderful organisation that works in the HIV education and treatment sector in South Africa. Almost all of the counsellors, health care workers and trainers who work in the organisation are, in my opinion, adult children. Their deep feelings of responsibility to those around them, their ability to see the best in people and their empathy and compassion are some of the qualities that have drawn them to the work and the context that they are involved in every day. Were it not for their troubled childhoods, they may well all be working in very different institutions and sectors, and the communities that they work with and support would not have had access to the services and care that these dedicated people offer every day.

Adult children have developed a strong self-reliance which means that we are often able to do things – even very difficult tasks – without assistance. Our issues with authority can translate into a gift for entrepreneurship and/or a need to work with autonomy in the workplace. Adult children are extremely able, very resilient and can handle a lot.

As you now know, the vast majority of my clients are adult children, and many of them are entrepreneurs. Even those in full-time employment generally have plans to work for themselves, or have small businesses on the side.

Adult children are usually very generous, and are driven to give to others, especially those they see as being less fortunate than themselves. The giving may be physical, emotional or material. Adult children are quick to recognise other people's distress and respond to it.

Too Much of Anything ...

Adult children are generally very intuitive and highly empathic. All those years of anticipating events, and reading moods and undercurrents in order to create diversions, makes them very tuned in to atmosphere and sub-text. Just like animals can 'feel' thunder in the air way before we humans can hear it, adult children can sense the way the people around them are feeling, often before those people are aware of their own feelings. While this gift can be pretty exhausting, used effectively, it can greatly enhance the experience of the adult child and the people with whom they work and live. It is particularly beneficial for adult children who work in any profession that involves people: healing, talking, listening, caring or teaching.

This gift can, however, become a little overwhelming, particularly as adult children struggle with boundaries at the best of times. Often, it needs a conscious decision and action to remain 'boundaried' in order not to absorb the emotions and feelings of the people around them. Judith Orloff, who speaks of 'intuitive empaths', has studied and observed how some people are able to 'catch' emotions such as fear, anger, sadness and frustration from those around them.

She calls such people 'emotional sponges' which is a good description for adult children. Not only do we often experience feelings of anxiety, fear and sadness ourselves, we also find it far too easy to pick up feelings and emotions belonging to other people, because our own emotional defences are already compromised.

Squeeze Out Your Sponge

When you are next aware of feelings of anxiety or disquiet, try and work out if the feelings belong to you or to someone else. You may have just left a friend or relative and be carrying their anger or depression away with you without even realising it. Adult children often take on other people's emotional business as well as their concrete business. If it is not your emotional business, get out of it.

If it is possible, take yourself away from anyone whose negative emotions you may be feeling. Try to step away from the person, or leave the room if you can, to put some physical distance between you and them. Then you will be less likely to take on their feelings. This can be as simple as taking a few steps back from the person. If it is not possible to remove yourself from the situation entirely, try to breathe deeply when in the presence of someone whose emotions you are absorbing, in order to get rid of the negativity that may not belong to you.

Being aware of if and how you may take on other peoples' fears, emotions and problems can help you to mindfully choose how you respond to others.

Out of the Darkness ...

'Although they are dark and dangerous, it is in the woods that we discover our strengths,' writes Elizabeth Lesser so beautifully in her book *Broken Open*. There are so many gifts that come from a childhood that is imperfect (and a lifetime of making sense of that childhood), the trick is in allowing ourselves to recognise them, and to move forward in and out of the woods.

See Yourself

Having a chaotic childhood certainly has its downsides, but it also results in some good stuff! Most adult children are very sensitive, very faithful friends, intuitive, empathic and extremely reliable. What are some of the other character traits that you have that you, or other people, appreciate in you?

When you can identify some of the gifts that your childhood has given you, you will be able to celebrate it, and celebrate life.

Giving Yourself a Green Light

Adult children can – often without knowing it – allow their pasts to predict their futures. Their fears and limiting beliefs can get in the way of all that they are capable of achieving (and, as we know, they are capable of achieving a lot) because these may translate into conflicting thoughts and beliefs about what they should or should not be doing. Often adult children hold themselves back from reaching their full potential because they have limiting expectations of themselves, or they are not sure they are deserving, or because they unconsciously fear change or fear upsetting the people around them ...

In her book *STOP Self-Sabotage* Pat Pearson gives a delightful description of self-sabotage: '... it is how we trip ourselves up when we are running to the finish line'. We can dream and scheme, and make plans and set goals, but we can't get what we want if we don't believe that we deserve it. There needs to be alignment and congruence between what we believe we can have and what we want to have, in order to get it. Adult children, many of whom are conditioned to expect bad things and disappointments in order to be prepared for any eventuality and to protect themselves from subsequent disappointment, find it hard to truly trust that they, too, can get good things, or that they will achieve their dreams.

People, particularly fearful people, frequently act out or precipitate their own worst fears. If they fear not being good enough, they will act not good enough. If they fear not being loved, they will seek out people who are unloving to be with. If they fear being left, they will leave first. Unfortunately, the more energy and attention we give to our fears, the more real we make them, and the more likely they are to happen to us.

Pearson describes five sabotage strategies: *resignation, denial, throwing it away, settling for less*, and *the fatal flaw*. All five of these strategies are applicable to adult children who are often expert self-saboteurs.

Resignation refers to giving up before we even start something; just not even going there. The need to be perfect or good enough often stops us from starting anything new. For adult children, the 'learning' period that applies to most people does not come into play – we should be experts even before we start. So, despite the best intentions to start gym or a new sport, we often do not get to the starting line because we have talked ourselves out of it.

Jane had wanted to unleash her creative side for some time, and after much searching found an art teacher who offered classes at a perfect time for her. Full of excitement she went to a trial class, sure that she would sign up for the lessons. When she got there, however, and saw the paintings that were being produced by the members of the class, she quickly became disillusioned. 'I can't paint like that,' she shrugged in explanation for why she didn't think she would be going back. Without really thinking about it, she had assumed that everyone else was able to paint like an experienced artist the very first time they ever picked up a paintbrush, and knowing that she wouldn't be able to do that made her give up before she had even started.

Denial manifests when self-saboteurs either don't allow themselves to see potential or existing problems, or don't take responsibility for their own role in a problem. Adult children are more likely to exhibit the former rather than the latter, and deny that things should be different in relationships, or work, or any area of their lives. Denial of and ignoring warning signals often results in negative and self-destructive patterns being repeated in love and at work. Otherscentered people are especially good at denial. They can spend years or decades refusing to see the truth about their relationships.

Throwing it away is another favourite of many adult children. This refers to the particular talent of leaving a person or situation before they are the ones to be left. The fear of being rejected is so strong that adult children may either be the rejecters, or they may not allow themselves to follow their dreams and reach their potential. They are scared that if they change and succeed then they will be left.

We may also throw away opportunities either before they have presented themselves, or when there is a very real possibility of them materialising.

Zelda was very good at throwing things away. Because her fear of not being good enough was so strong, when she was invited to accept an award that was being given to her company in recognition of the contribution that she in large part was responsible for making, she thought she may ask her boss to go to the ceremony instead.

'Why would you not want to go yourself?' I asked in some confusion, having heard for some weeks how hard she had worked on that particular project. Her answer was that she was afraid that someone might ask her to make a speech or answer a question she would not be prepared for. Rather than risking the humiliation she was certain she would experience, she wanted to give her glory away to someone else.

Zelda had another 'throwing it away' habit, too. When a colleague whom she had loved from afar for a very long time started to make it clear that he was interested in seeing her romantically, she became so anxious about him getting to know her that she turned him down flat when he asked her out on a date.

Settling for less is also deeply ingrained in many adult children, who put up with leftovers, expect the worst so that they won't be disappointed, and/or don't try so that they won't fail.

Priscilla yearned for someone she could share her life with, someone who would make her feel special and treat her well. But she was so worn down by disappointment and her limiting expectations about what she deserves, that she kept herself at home whenever she was not at work. Then, unexpectedly, she met a man at a friend's house. He was wonderful – clever, kind, charming and successful. And married. Which made him even more irresistible.

Having a relationship with a married person is the personification of settling for less. It was just one aspect of Priscilla's propensity to put up with leftovers. The job that she hated but didn't think she should change because she should be grateful to have any job at all, was another manifestation of her self-sabotage.

The fatal flaw is a more subtle sabotage strategy as it refers to something in the person's nature which gets in the way of success. Often, people will be on their way to achieving a goal, when a Survivor Self belief or a negative behaviour pattern will kick in and will prevent them from getting there. With adult children, our unconscious beliefs and fears may cause us to procrastinate ourselves to a standstill, or abort a plan of action if we think that it will not be as perfect as we want it to be. Other ways that we self-sabotage include taking on too much, not telling ourselves the truth about what we really want, and pushing ourselves into exhaustion and burnout. There is no doubt that adult children have a propensity for self-sabotage.

Self-rescue

I believe that we also have a great propensity for self-rescue. Our Survivor Self, so attuned to our unconscious fears and requirements, often steps in quietly and stealthily to rescue us from something that we do not really want to do, or that is bad for us.

And, being adult children, we are quick to beat ourselves up for tripping ourselves up when, actually, we are just stopping ourselves from making a terrible mistake.

Priya had just resigned from a job she had had for ten years and was setting herself up as a freelance consultant. An ex-colleague, Brian, had invited her to join him in submitting a tender for a very large government contract. They worked on the proposal for weeks, crossing all the Ts and dotting all the Is until it was perfect. It ticked all the boxes and they were sure to be in the running to get the job. Priya offered to take the tender document to the government office and hand it in on the appointed day. The tender box closed at 12pm. Priya got there at 12:01pm. The box was closed, and no amount of crying and begging would get the guardian of the tender box to let her hand in her package.

Priya was devastated. She came for coaching because she wanted help understanding 'why I always sabotage myself'. During the course of our first session, it emerged that Priya didn't really want to do the work that winning the tender would have entailed. She had only said yes to Brian because she didn't want to say no to the tender, in case he never asked her to work on another one with him. Faced with the very real possibility that she would have to spend many months doing work that felt excruciating, Priya's Survivor Self stepped in and rescued her by making sure the tender never got granted to her.

The great thing about both self-sabotage and self-rescue, is that when we become aware of what we are doing, we can choose to respond differently. So, Jane was brave and went back to the art class and has discovered that she loves it and she is steadily getting better at her painting. Zelda went to the awards ceremony, sat next to the handsome colleague, and allowed him to get to know her sufficiently to ask her out on another date, even though he was now aware that she was not perfect. Priscilla realised that accepting someone else's leftovers was not good enough for her and she extricated herself from the married man, and successfully applied for a scholarship to study what she really wanted to. Priya had an honest conversation with Brian about what kind of tenders she was interested in working on with him.

How do you sabotage or rescue yourself? Look at the areas of your life you struggle with and see which sabotage or rescue strategies you use in each. Then think about ways that you can make sure your shoelaces are firmly tied so that you can be sure to cross that finish line.

The ability to identify and name these self-sabotage and self-rescue strategies will allow you to recognise the negative behaviour and address it. Underlying all of these self-limiting tactics are the limiting beliefs and fears and survival strategies that you developed to protect yourself, but that probably no longer serve you.

We need to be vigilant about noticing when the limiting beliefs and the negative self-talk creep in, in order to come to believe that we CAN do and be what we want.

Stepping Out

I cannot count the number of clients I have had who have known that they want to make a change to their lives, and often even known what they wanted that change to be. But the thought of actually making a change is paralysing to them.

Adult children are often plagued by ambivalence about change in their lives. On the one hand, they want to improve things, but on the other hand they fear losing control and entering unpredictable waters again.

I believe – and I see evidence to support this belief regularly – that ambivalence is the single biggest stumbling block to our progress. We can think, feel and believe that we want to make a change in our lives, we can be totally convinced that it is the right thing for us, but if there is any hint of ambivalence, we will not achieve that change. We are ambivalent when we have mixed feelings about something; part of us wants it, and another part of us doesn't.

Ntombi wanted to lose weight. For years she had tried every diet that came across her path. She would lose a couple of kilograms and then put them right back on. She would start a fitness regime and, as soon as she started making headway, she would abandon it. She was extremely frustrated and cross when she came for coaching. I gave her the 'what is holding you back?' exercise (you will find it on the following page) to complete. After writing for 15 minutes she started to laugh through the tears that had begun to roll down her cheeks. 'I've just realised that I'm scared of losing weight because everyone will expect me to become different. I'll have to change how I dress, become more productive and assertive at work, I'll probably even be expected to trade my car in for a fancier one.'

Ntombi made the startling discovery that, for all those years, she had been terrified that losing weight would make her more visible and put more pressure on her to perform. Although a part of her truly wanted to shed a few kilograms, there was a larger part of her that feared that she would be expected to change who she was in order to fit in with her new size.

With all powerful thoughts that impede our happiness and progress, it is the unconscious nature of the ambivalence that makes it so powerful. Until we are aware that we have mixed feelings about something, we cannot work out what we are fearful of, and cannot reassure ourselves that we will manage to successfully address it.

What is Holding You Back?

Identify something that you have thought about for some time — something that you would really like to achieve or to have happen in your life. Maybe you can start small with something like starting an exercise regime, eating more healthily or visiting your parents regularly. When you get the hang of the exercise you can move on to bigger issues such as work or relationships. It is very helpful to do this exercise by writing free-hand and for as long as possible for each answer.

Write down your goal.

Now write down the answers to the following questions:

- ★ Why do you want to achieve this goal?
- ★ What will the benefits be?
- ★ Will there be any drawbacks?
- ★ What are you scared of in reaching this goal?
- ★ How will your life change?
- ★ How will your relationships be affected?

As honestly as possible, answer all of these questions by writing a half-page answer for each in your journal.

Look at all the answers you have written, and highlight any words or phrases that show feelings of lack of certainty or ambivalence – anything that you have identified that makes the achievement of that goal seem to be possibly less than altogether easy and beneficial. These are the thoughts that are holding you back.

How can you turn them around to help you to achieve your goals? Ask yourself if the thoughts that are holding you back are fear based or reality based? My guess is that the vast majority – if not all – of them will be fear based. So, be brave, tell yourself the truth and take the plunge!

A Word on Gratitude

The society we find ourselves in is very good at making us aware of what we do not have, but not always so focused on encouraging us to acknowledge all the good things we do have. Being depressed or in the habit of paying attention to lack and disappointment may also make us less able to see the positives around us. But the more we allow ourselves to recognise and appreciate the good, the more good we start to notice.

Gratitude is the experience of a positive emotion or attitude in appreciation of good things that we receive, or know we will receive. One of the most powerful strategies for moving forward into a better life is the regular practice of gratitude.

Awareness of gratitude and its benefits has been growing over the last decade. Recent research suggests that people who are more grateful are happier and experience more well-being. They are less depressed, less stressed and more satisfied with their lives and their relationships. Grateful people also appear to have greater control of their environments, their life purpose and their acceptance of self, and are better able to ask for and to receive help and support. They are more likely to learn and grow from difficulties that they experience, and are better able to plan how to respond to problems.

Grateful people also have fewer negative coping strategies, and are therefore less likely to try and avoid the problem or deny there is a problem, blame themselves, or cope through substance use and abuse. And, it seems, they sleep better!

Gratitude Practice

Many people have a daily gratitude practice (Oprah is one of them) and I encourage you to do the same. You can easily combine this with your morning pages which I also encourage you to make part of your daily routine. All you need to do is every day, think about – and again it helps to write these down – five things for which you are grateful. They do not have to be particularly earth shattering. They might look like this: Today I am grateful for the sunshine, for the perfect cup of coffee I am drinking, for seeing my best friend for lunch, for the bird singing outside my window, and for feeling happy.

It is a very powerful, simple and effective practice and I can't recommend it highly enough.

See the good

Putting our attention on positive things and that for which we are grateful makes us more likely to see all the other positive things that are around us, and to experience life more joyfully and peacefully. It is particularly effective to think about people who you are grateful to for being in your life, but is also helps to think about anything else for which you would like to give thanks: weather, pets, trees, chocolate – whatever adds value to your personal world

In a similar vein, it is helpful to put our attention on the things we would like to bring into our lives. Law of Attraction, manifesting, visualisation, call it what you will, there's no doubt that when we are clear about what we want to bring into our lives, it is easier to do that. I often have clients tell me they want to leave their job, but when I ask them what kind of work they would prefer to be doing, they have no idea. It is not enough to know what we are leaving behind. We also need to know what we are moving toward if we are to be sure that it will be better for us. The clearer we can be about what we want, the better the chances are of us achieving it.

Have a Vision

You have spent loads of time understanding where you come from and where you are in your life. Now it is time to plan where you would like to go, and a vision board is a wonderful way to do this. It is fun and creative without being threatening. You don't have to draw your own pictures, unless you want to, of course. Just cut them out of magazines.

The idea is that if you surround yourself with images of what you want to do, where you want to go and how you want to be (and who you want to be with), your life will change to match those images and meet your desires. Vision boards add clarity and feelings to your hopes and dreams. And they are fun to make – on your own or with friends.

Gather as many different magazines as possible, some cardboard, scissors and glue, and a photo of yourself looking happy and well. Put some gentle music on, spend a few minutes setting your intention – thinking about why you are doing the exercise – and then get cracking! Without thinking too much, tear out any images, phrases or words that catch your eye in the magazines. When you have a healthy pile and have gone through all your magazines, choose the ones you want to stick on the vision board, and decide how you want them to be placed, remembering to keep a space for your photo. Then stick them all down, taking care not to leave any empty spaces on the cardboard. Design your vision board to reflect the abundance you want to have in your life. Stick the board up somewhere where you will see it every day, and wait to see how your dreams come true.

With increased awareness of the thoughts and actions that have been holding you back, clearer ideas of where you want to go, and the tools and strength developed through this journey, I believe that you can take yourself anywhere and everywhere that you want to go. Now that you can see it, you can make it happen.

Thanks to YOU

We have undergone quite a journey together and I would like to end off by thanking you for your bravery and your commitment to yourself. It has been difficult in some places, I'm sure, and you have persevered and worked hard. Not only do I want to thank you, I also want you to thank yourself.

Thank yourself for this journey and for all your gifts and strengths. Thank yourself for the bravery you have shown your whole life, and for your resilience and your strength. Thank yourself for growing into who you are, and who you are still to become.

Give yourself permission to make new choices and to let your light shine.

Bibliography

Beattie, M. (1992) *Codependent No More. How to Stop Controlling Others and Start Caring For Yourself.* Hazelden, USA.

Beck, M. (2008) *Steering by Starlight: How to Fulfil Your Destiny, No Matter What.* Piatkus, UK.

Black, C. (1981) *It Will Never Happen To Me!* Random House, USA.

Cameron, J. (1993) *The Artist's Way: A Course in Discovering and Recovering your Creative Self.* Pan, UK.

Cameron, J. (2004) *The Sound of Paper.* Michael Joseph, Great Britain.

Hallowell, E.N. (2004) *Dare to Forgive: The Power of Letting Go and Moving On.* HCI, USA.

http://www.drjudithorloff.com/Free-Articles/how-to-stop-absorbing.htm

http://www.guesswhatnormalis.com/2007/05/play_to_your_st.html

Katie, B. (21 May 2009) *Staying in Your Own Business,* from http://www.sageera.com/articles/comments/staying_in_your_own_business/

Kritsberg, W. (1988) *The Adult Children of Alcoholics Syndrome: A step-by-step guide to discovery and recovery.* Bantam Books, USA.

Lesser, E. (2004) *Broken Open.* Rider Books, London.

Norwood, R. (2004) *Women Who Love Too Much.* Arrow Books, London.

Pearson, P. (2009) *Stop Self-Sabotage: Get Out of Your Way to Earn More Money, Improve Your Relationships and Find the Success You Deserve*. McGraw-Hill, USA.

Whitfield, C.D. (1987) *Healing The Child Within*. Health Communications, Florida.

Whitfield, C.D. (1990) *A Gift to Myself; A Personal Workbook and Guide to Healing My Child Within*. Health Communications, Florida.

Woititz, J.G. (2002) *The Complete ACOA Sourcebook: Adult Children of Alcoholics at Home, at Work and in Love*. Health Communications, Florida.

http://www.guesswhatnormalis.com/2008/09/feedback-taking.html

http://www.guesswhatnormalis.com/2009/04/authority-figure-issues.html

www.LawofAttractionBook.com

www.recoverymatters.co.za